1. The Life of St. Claude de la Colombiere

Francis, O.S.B.

The Life of St. Claude de la Colombiere

St. Claude was canonized
by Pope John Paul II
on May 31, 1992.

~~~~~~

Read also: The Spiritual Direction of
St. Claude de la Colombière

Translated & arranged by
Mother M. Philip, I.B.V.M.
The Bar Convent, York
[Ignatius Press - San Francisco]

The Life of
ST. CLAUDE
DE LA COLOMBIERE

Spiritual Director of St. Margaret Mary

RUTH H. LaVIGNE

St. Paul Books & Media

Library of Congress Cataloging-in-Publication Data

LaVigne, Ruth H.
   The Life of St. Claude de la Colombiere : spiritual director of
St. Margaret Mary / Ruth H. LaVigne.
      p.   cm.
   Rev. ed. of : Special messenger, c1978.
   ISBN 0-8198-4467-5
   1. La Colombiere, Claude de, Saint, 1641-1682. 2. Catholic
Church — Clergy — Biography.   I. LaVigne, Ruth H.
Special messenger.   II. Title.   III. Title: Life of Saint Claude
de la Colombiere.
   BX4705.C689L37   1992
   282'.092 — dc20
   [B]   92-12736
                                                                  CIP

(Original title: *Special Messenger*)

Published in the U.S.A. by St. Paul Books & Media,
50 St. Paul's Avenue, Boston, MA 02130.

St. Paul Books & Media is the publishing house of the Daughters of St.
Paul, an international congregation of women religious serving the Church
with the communications media.

Current Printing - first digit 1 2 3 4 5 6 7 8 9 10

          99   98   97   96   95   94   93   92

*One of the saints said that the
priesthood is the love of the Sacred Heart.
This little story is affectionately
dedicated to Msgr. Robert J. McCarthy,
whose priesthood, like Saint Claude's,
has been spent in promoting the love
of the Sacred Heart.*

Contents

1.

The Archer

THE minute Claude awoke, he tumbled out of bed and ran to the window. On the slope of the hill below he saw the colored roofs of houses and shops spread out like a giant quilt. From hundreds of chimneys all over the city, blue and gray smoke from breakfast fires curled up lazily in the still air of this autumn morning in 1650. Claude frowned. He saw that the gate at the end of the garden was still shut tight.

Claude could always tell when his father had come or gone, for he never quite closed the gate. Everyone else did, because Mother insisted on it but Father always said there were "more important things to think about."

"What could be keeping him so long?" Claude wondered as he threw his smock over his head and ran downstairs to breakfast, tying a sash around his waist.

"Mother, Mother! When will Father be back from Lyons? Will he come back this morning?"

Marguerite de la Colombiere, his mother, did not answer at once but went on stirring porridge in a steaming kettle. "When he's finished his business, very likely." Then she turned and faced him with a sad look on her young face.

"Claude, you know we love having you tutored right here in the house with us, don't you?"

"Of course, Mother! But when will Father be back?" Why was she talking like this?

Marguerite and her son were not thinking of the same things.

"Claude, dear, when I think how young you are! Nine years old last spring; and here we've scarcely lived in Vienne a year! Before noon your Father will be back. How will you feel if he says you have to leave us and go to school in Lyons in October?"

Now it was Claude's turn to be silent. He glanced at her with a puzzled look. Then he turned his head toward the window facing north and gazed out over the Rhone Valley. He wasn't sure how he felt about going away to school. Lyons seemed so strange and distant. It was really only a name to him, that city in the mountains, twenty miles beyond the horizon. He'd never been so far from home. And for eight long months — he would come home only for Christmas. Being away from one's family at the age of nine was not to be thought of lightly. It was an awesome prospect.

Until this year he had been too ill to walk two miles back and forth to day school with his brothers, Humbert and Floris. So he stayed at home and was tutored by Pere Dupree, who came for an hour each day. Claude was satisfied to be able to study all day with his mother. She was always near enough so that he could find her when he felt the need to talk something over. And his father? He was a lawyer who had to spend most of his time away working on law cases. Yes, leaving his mother would be the hardest thing Claude had ever done.

He knew it would be even harder for his mother. Even he could sense that. She was close to her children, seeming to make up to them for their father's absences.

Yet, it would be so exciting. Lyons! What an adventure! The third largest city in France. To be all alone in such a place! What a lot of strange stories he had heard of the soldiers and traders who came there from all over the world! Yes, he would, for once, have tales to tell his brothers.

Claude began feeling a little guilty thinking this way. Finally his mother asked him again, "How will you feel if you have to leave us, Claude?" He didn't answer. Again he looked up quickly into her face with an expression of tenderness and uneasiness. Instead of speaking, he broke away and ran out into the yard yelling back, "Mother, have you seen Partisan? Has he gone to Lyons too?"

His mother stood in the doorway looking wearily after him. "Good heavens," she murmured, half smiling, "all he can think of is his dog!"

The very next moment, as Claude yanked open the gate, yelling, "Partisan, Partisan!" he saw in the path before him a tall form whose boots and cape were covered with dust.

"Will I do?" asked the man.

"Father, Father!" Claude threw his arms around his father's waist. Bertrand de la Colombiere's huge hands nearly covered his son's back. As he embraced the boy he looked up into the eyes of his wife, who stood in the doorway. Her smile did not hide the look of anxiety on her face.

"Claude," Bertrand de la Colombiere finally said, "I would like to speak to your mother."

"Wouldn't you like to speak to me?"

"Speak to you? Why, what on earth have I got to say to you?" Bertrand looked down at his son with a twinkle in his eye. "You, young man, are wanted by your brothers for an expedition to Mount Salamont today. I'll see *you* when you return."

"But there's no expedition to Salamont today, Father."

"There *will* be in fifteen minutes, *mon ami*," he replied. So saying, he took his son's hand, then his wife's, and followed them into the kitchen for breakfast.

Having his coffee and buttered rolls in silence, Bertrand watched his wife getting a picnic lunch together for her sons. Into a leather bag went grapes from their vineyard in back, a long loaf of fresh bread, cheese, a honeycomb, and a green glass bottle of goat's milk. Claude was outside again looking for Partisan. His brothers were dressing upstairs.

"Marguerite, help me decide what to do," Bertrand said. "I've been to see the Jesuits in Lyons. I find Bon Secours an excellent school. You know yourself that the Jesuits themselves are everywhere called the 'schoolmasters of Europe'; and they teach the very subjects most valuable to a boy going on to study law: Latin, logic and public speaking. Still, I cannot make up my mind whether to send him or not."

"I suppose you are worried about how I feel," Marguerite said.

"I suppose I am. How do you feel about it, Marguerite?"

She knew he would ask her one day, so she gave him her answer. She had pondered long over it.

"I think Claude should have the best education he can get."

Bertrand looked at her as though weighing her tone of voice with her words.

"Thank you, Marguerite," he said slowly, "but how do you really feel?"

She bowed her head, not daring to look at him. Then she said, "I think he should go to Lyons — but not right away."

"Ah!" was all Bertrand said. Her compromise perplexed him. One of the strongest reasons he had for sending Claude away was precisely to keep him from becoming so attached to his mother that he would never leave. But how could he tell her this? All he could think of was, "You know, my dear, I think Claude ought to see more of the world."

"Do you mean 'less of his mother?'"

Now it was Bertrand's turn to be silent so Marguerite answered her own question.

"I know, Bertrand, it means 'less of his father,' too. And this means as much to you as to me. So I will let you decide. Whatever you do, I know you will be just and not selfish."

Within half an hour, Claude pulled the tailgate shut, the latch falling into place with a clank. With his brothers Humbert and Floris, aged fifteen and seven, Claude headed down the narrow, cobblestoned streets toward the river below. With them was Parti-

san, who made a pest of himself as usual, yapping at every passing
cart. This was embarrassing to Claude, who was sensitive to what
people thought of him. It was not Partisan, but Claude, who felt the
stream of abuse when the dog was caught sniffing the pigs that hung
outside the meatshop.

"Get out of here with that mutt," bellowed the butcher, "or I'll
hang you both up here for sale!" Claude cringed. Humbert shouted
something unflattering about the butcher's resemblance to the pigs.
Away they fled, Partisan excitedly leading, till they reached the
river. Children and dog were caught up in a spirit of high adventure
such as only boys and their dogs can achieve in a free and bouncy
fashion.

On the river beside them, barges drifted slowly by. After a few
days, if the crews were lucky enough to avoid the sand bars, they
would reach Avignon and then the Mediterranean, where their
barrels of oil and bolts of silk would be loaded on ships for ports all
over the world. The bargemen waved at the boys, and the boys waved
back. The barges came from Lyons, and they were going to the ends
of the earth! Everything reminded Claude of Lyons, and Lyons made
him think, "It is so much fun going on hikes with my brothers. I
wonder if I could bear to leave it all?"

As they followed the riverbank and finally reached the edge of
the city, Claude was so wrapped up in daydreams and memories that
he hardly noticed where they were going. Humbert pointed out the
historic sites to his younger brother, Floris, who had trouble because
of tripping over the edges of his hand-me-down pants. As they passed
the Benedictine Abbey nestled among the ruins, Claude began
listening. But what did he care about those stones scattered about the
cloister foundations, which had belonged to an old temple in Roman
times? This was no time for history! Claude couldn't care less about
the fact that Julius Caesar himself had once camped on the hilltop
above their house. Now this was suddenly in the past. All Claude
could think of was the future, and especially the immediate future.

"Tonight I shall know, tonight I shall know!" That evening loomed bright with exciting possibilities.

They passed the city walls through North Gate and on out into the countryside, all golden under the September sun. The wind swept down from the Alps and, like an invisible comb, bent the tall wheat first to one side and then to the other. The boys followed the old Roman Road till it brought them parallel again with the mighty Rhone River.

Humbert knew well enough that his mission today was not to amuse Claude especially, but to keep the house clear and quiet while his mother and father talked. Just the same, he carried an enormous bow in one hand and a fistful of arrows in the other.

"You never can tell *what* you'll meet on the way," he explained to Floris, who jumped up and down so much with excitement that he nearly lost his trousers.

Soon the little band was struggling up the goat path that zigzagged up the side of Mount Salamont. Humbert used his bow for a walking stick. He tired quickly, and soon stopped to rest. Looking downhill he could see Claude wheezing and puffing as he clambered up the rocks.

"Hurry, Claude!" he yelled. "We'll wait for you." The others were glad for an excuse to rest. Soon they were climbing together again, but by the time they reached the top, Claude was coughing wretchedly. Still, he felt a little proud of himself. Never until today had he been able to make the entire climb. He had always turned back earlier. Now, even a trip to Lyons didn't seem too far.

From their perch high above the lush green and gold valley, the horizon spread out around them with houses and trees looking like toys. Claude gazed with fascination at the distant countryside. He never tired of the river and the hills, for each time he looked he noticed something new. He always saw more than anyone else.

Claude shivered at the massive bulk of the Alps to the east, seeing Mont Blanc gleaming all white in its eternal snows, only ninety miles away. Then, looking upriver, he saw the cluster of

houses that was the town of St. Symphorien d'Ozon where he had
been born and had lived until a year ago. Upriver further still, where
the Rhone was met by the Saone coming down from the north, stood
Lyons itself. The city sparkled through a bluish haze that had
gathered around its hills. Ah! there it was! The glitter of stone and
glass!

It was time for lunch, he realized, when the sun was high and
his stomach began to feel empty. In between munches of bread and
cheese, Humbert told Floris stories about wars and the Roman
Emperors who had lived in this neighborhood. Claude heard them
talking of Trajan, who had built his forum atop Fourviere in Lyons,
and how Emperor Claudius had lived there later, before he went
north to make Britain a Roman province. More history! Couldn't they
think of the present, or of tomorrow?

Humbert turned to Claude teasingly, "Well, now, maybe you
get your name from Emperor Claudius." "From a pagan emperor?"
Claude shot back. "I hope not!" Humbert knew he could get his
young brother to provide entertainment for their lunch hour. He
loved to goad him into giving speeches, and Claude loved giving
them.

"Come on," Humbert said, "I can't see what's so shameful
about being named after an emperor, pagan or otherwise. After all,
don't we owe the most to the pagans who came here to Vienne and
civilized the ancient Gauls? Look down there. There's the Roman
road we came on today. It'll be here centuries after we're gone!"

"What!" Claude broke in. "We owe nothing to the pagans! We
owe everything to the Christians. They made Vienne civilized when
they came here and made it their first outpost beyond the Alps."

Now that the young preacher was getting under way, Humbert
leaned back lazily, grinning, with his hands behind his head, and
gazed at the clouds racing by close over them.

As he spoke, Claude struck poses he had seen Pere Dupree use
at Sunday Mass: "Look there," he said, "ten steeples for every
Roman column!" Turning to Floris and Humbert, who were not

looking, Claude pointed his finger accusingly at them. "You! You talk about emperors! Saints have walked where we walked this afternoon! Lazarus for one. He came here in the days after our Lord raised him from the dead. Mary Magdalene for another. She lived right here in Vienne."

Humbert went on grinning, his eyes peacefully closed. Claude was annoyed. He turned to Floris, who squatted on the edge of a stone, fascinated by his brother's eloquence.

"Do you know who may have sat where you're sitting?"

Floris shook his head to say, "No."

"Do you know who came all the way from Jerusalem, banished by his emperor, Augustus, to commit suicide right over there off the edge of the cliff, not ten steps from where I'm standing?"

Floris shook his head more vigorously than before as if to say, "No, who?" His eyes blinked as Claude cast a swordlike gesture to the brink.

"None other than Pontius Pilate!"

At this flourish Humbert and Floris were delighted and burst into applause.

"Hurray! Well then," said Humbert, "I suppose we'd better call you 'Pontius de la Colombiere.' There's a mouthful!"

Claude frowned as the others laughed. He knew a way to turn the tables on them. "The reason that Caesar was a great general was not that he was a big man," he remembered Pere Dupree saying.

"All right, Humbert. If you're so fond of your pagan heroes, take your bow and show us how they would have landed an arrow on attackers coming along the road down there."

Humbert looked down. The road was a long way down and a longer way out, it seemed. Nevertheless, he scowled, took up his bow, drew back the arrow and let it fly. "Whu-ung!" went the string, and the arrow arched out gracefully, then down and down till it buried itself in a bush halfway down the slope. Humbert was silent.

"Tsk, tsk," was all that Claude said. He waited for Floris to try, but his arrow barely cleared the wall that circled the summit of the old medieval fort. Then Claude tried. He reached for the bow, which was too long for anyone his age, and took the longest of the remaining arrows. Lying on his back, he placed his feet on the wall, the bow hooked under his toes, the arrow between his legs, and heaving back on the string with both hands, he sent the willow stick singing on its way toward the road. The arc was graceful, Claude thought, scrambling to his feet, and they all cheered loudly as the arrow plunged beyond the road into the dust at the edge of the field.

Suddenly they stopped shouting. Who should appear below them coming around the bend heading for Vienne but Pere Dupree, their Latin and Greek teacher, black as a crow in his soutane and broad-rimmed hat, reading his breviary.

The snap of an arrow struck his ears — a puff of dust blew up in the wind not twenty feet in front of him. He looked up just in time to see heads disappear behind the wall on the hilltop.

"Hallo-o, you barbarians!" he bellowed. "I know how to deal with you! Look down there. I've sent a company of horses to rout you out!" With that, he picked up the broken shaft and continued his stately walk toward Vienne.

The boys looked south, and saw the glimmer of shields. A column of cavalry was plodding back to quarters in Lyons from the war in Spain. Crouched out of sight, the little band of popeyed "barbarians" could distinguish in the wind the distant sound of hoofs, the whinnying of the horses and the shouts of the sergeants above the soldiers' lusty song. (If Pere Dupree could hear that song, Claude thought, he would have changed his mind as to who the barbarians were.) They saw the citizens rushing to greet the soldiers as they cantered into the square, with banners of fleur-de-lis, white against blue, fluttering out ahead of the riders. Humbert leaped up and ran down the path to greet them, too.

Floris ran down with Humbert. Claude wanted to linger for a last look at the horizon. Watching his brothers get smaller on the hillside, he thought of the excitement of talking with the soldiers again, of hearing their stories of hand-to-hand battle, which he imagined to be so dreadful, but so fascinating. Some might spend the night with their family, and Claude could help his mother change bandages, as she had taught all her children to do.

As Claude watched the enormous white mass of the mountain range turning a faint ember-glow in the setting sun, he wondered at Humbert's enthusiasm. He never seemed to tire of hearing of war. Even hearing of the discoveries in New France, it was never the work of the explorers and missionaries, but always the gory details of the tortures by the Indian savages that made his brother pester the teachers for more. It was very exciting, and the men who suffered physically were certainly heroes, especially those who died. "But wasn't there something more to being great?" Claude often wondered. "Couldn't a man be great somehow, even if he were physically weak?"

He glanced quickly to the north. Lyons was growing darker now in a mysterious haze. Lyons! He'd nearly forgotten! The sooner he got home, the sooner he'd know. So he climbed up over the wall and followed his brothers down the path.

At the bottom, Claude took the lead along a side route to the city. "Pere Dupree is a very nice man," Claude said, "the way he joked about the arrow and all. But let's not overtake him on the main road."

"Yes," Humbert agreed, grinning, "we might disturb him reading his Office, eh, Claude?"

"Besides," Floris piped up, "that arrow of yours nearly killed him, didn't it, Claude?"

"Quiet, Floris," Claude said, and he picked up the pace. "Let's not talk too long with the soldiers, all right?" He said over his shoulder. "And let's not talk at all about the arrow to Mother and Father, all right?"

"All right," everyone agreed.

Soon they were off under the long shadows of Vienne's North Gate. Then, as they rushed by the meat shop, Partisan kept close to Claude's heels.

2.

Soldiers

ON the way home Claude's head so spun with wonder over both his father's decision over Lyons and the sights that awaited him at home that he scarcely noticed how his heart was pounding, his legs throbbing, and his chest heaving. The nearer they came to the public square the more Claude suspected that his morning's anxiety over his future would look rather petty in contrast to the anxieties of hundreds of hungry, wounded men.

His suspicions were soon confirmed. In the Vienne square they met the army, as had everyone else in town. Humbert immediately recognized a soldier whom his family had helped the year before when some officers and aides had been billeted at their old house in St. Symphorien. Proudly, then, the boys returned home from their expedition in the company of Pierre (whose last name they could never remember but whose stories of battle they certainly did) and three of his wounded companions.

As the band of warriors, now grown to eight, turned the corner of the lane and walked toward their house, Claude could see that his return was not to be a triumph after all. Someone else had thought of helping the soldiers, too. In fact, it looked as if a whole company of horsemen had come to spend the night, for outside the open gate a dozen horses stood tethered to the fence posts, munching on the grass and the flowers within reach. The animals were dusty and sweaty and very hungry. One tall horse had reached over the fence to chew off great bunches of Madame de la Colombiere's gorgeous white mallow blossoms.

Inside the gate was pandemonium. Soldiers were everywhere. Many of them who were wounded were lying on their blankets on the ground. In a pile near the door were helmets and breastplates, the officers' swords and stacks of muskets, together with a few bows that had a cruel, professional look. As Humbert fingered them, he decided that their purpose was not limited to archery as a sport. Men who were able to walk were busy building fires under the tripods of their field kettles. Others were stooped over in the garden pulling out carrots and onions by the handful.

It was an altogether sorry sight, the boys were thinking, this aftermath of war. This was not so glorious. Last spring it had been different. Going to war was the time for stories. When the soldiers went toward Spain, the horses were fresh and spirited, the armor shining, and the men full of a sense that someone needed them badly. At least someone was going to pay them well, mercenaries that they were, most of them. Now, to a boy, everything and everybody seemed worn out, and for no visible purpose. Perhaps the king was better off for all those mud-stained bandages and for the state of that one man missing an arm on one side and a hand on the other.

Certainly the Colombiere family was no better for it. He could see some of the havoc. As he wandered about looking for his parents, Claude puzzled over this real side of life: could it be such a wonderful thing to kill a man that they should actually have played at war all afternoon? Could the real Roman soldiers ever have looked like these? The only thing wonderful about war now seemed to Claude to be the self-sacrifice of his parents in cleaning up some of war's stain and ruin. How much nobler it would be to teach against war and to work for peace than to lead men off to battle!

Now Claude had less stomach than ever for stories. He was eager to be with his parents and to watch what they were doing for these men. Let Humbert have his tales of war and glory, he thought. A vain, stupid business, this killing!

Neither Claude's mother nor father was anywhere to be seen. Indeed, most of the soldiers didn't even know who their hosts were. War was their business and this was just another house, not their own, in a town they were passing through. It was the business of the officers to see them provided for; "Let the officers make friends if they have to," their attitude seemed to be. So Claude had to run about the house until he found his mother on the terrace near the garden. She was dressed in a straw colored jumper splotched with red, bending over an officer, gently soaking strips of soiled linen from his shoulder.

"Go and get me some pieces of the old, soft linen scraps from the chest in the pantry. And bring a kettle of fresh warm water, Claude." They were the first words he heard. He ran to the kitchen, brimming with the joy of being useful. Back on the terrace he watched Marguerite take the soft cloth and dampen the dried blood that was causing the last pieces of bandage to adhere to the man's shoulder. Evidently it had been a deep sabre wound. Claude suddenly asked to be excused, for he saw the man writhe and heard him groan.

"Mamma, may I go down and look for Papa?" he asked. Before she could reply, he was gone. His mother looked up, smiling, and yet a little sad, as she watched his head and shoulders disappear down the steps. She had no stomach for this, either. But she stayed just the same. Her reason was simple enough: if she didn't stay, who would? The man might die. Other soldiers had died on the way back from Spain. The strength her faith gave her came simply enough, too. When not talking quietly to distract the wounded from their pain as she applied herb poultices and changed their bandages, she talked silently to God, just as though he were right there on the terrace — which he was, in the light of her faith. He was in every one of these men, so that really she was ministering to him, too.

Claude was glad to do any errand that could keep him from

having to watch the wounds too closely or too long. For a while he hauled water from the well to the kettles.

A brawny mess-sergeant stirred a soup kettle swung over an open fire. He had appropriated the Colombiere's carrots, some thyme and celery. With a measure of beans and some onions boiled all together, this would be the soldiers' supper for tonight. Claude watched the process with interest.

Claude next found it useful and distracting to run errands for the doctor. Herbs were good, this officer said, for soothing stomachs upset by drinking the river water in Spain. So Claude went from house to house among the neighbors to ask for the herbs that were needed when Mother's supply was used up.

As long as Claude could keep moving he enjoyed it. "Charity" was all right, he thought, but you had to enjoy it, too. Would he be a doctor? No, never. That was clear. How else could he help the poor? He would have to think about it. If they were too poor it might be very, very difficult. There were many of those right in Vienne, whose hovels and shacks he couldn't bear to enter, let alone work in or live in. Anyway, for now, it was something new to be helping at all. To think that only this morning he had been entirely preoccupied with thoughts of himself. What a difference!

Claude's father noticed this, despite all the things he had on his mind. He had been dispatching his sons on one errand after another, yet he couldn't help noticing how responsive they were to the voices that called out to them, often in pain. Meeting his wife by chance as they passed in the yard, each carrying logs for the fires, Bertrand stopped Marguerite for a moment to rest.

"Look there," he said, pointing with a nod of his head toward Claude and Floris, who were carefully stepping over the bandaged legs and around the fires to bring soup to the soldiers, "They haven't eaten yet themselves. You know, I think that tonight they are passing from childhood into manhood."

Marguerite looked him abruptly in the face. "What! Not eaten yet?" she cried. "Well, if that's the case, for the love of heaven, let's feed them!"

Then, more self-contained, and solicitously: "Please do," she smiled, "unless you want their manhood to end in the morning and their eternal life to begin with the sunrise."

She was half teasing him, which he rather liked, though he pretended to be hurt.

"The trouble with you," he said, "is that you haven't the soul for the important things in life."

"So! Since you know what is important, I'll leave the fuel to you!" Marguerite tossed her head like a piqued schoolgirl, dropped her logs at the door for her husband to pick up, and went off to feed her sons. Really, she was thinking, how helpful it was that her husband could manage to keep alive the whole family's sense of humor even in their most serious moments. "Life becomes quite weighty," he had been known to say, "if you take yourself seriously all the time."

Humbert seemed to have learned this lightness of heart from his father, to judge from the way his mother found him. There he was, soup bowl on his knee, laughing with some soldiers sitting near one of the fires as he listened to their stories. He also seemed to have learned laziness from someone, but Marguerite couldn't imagine from whom. Bertrand had said once that he had made it up all by himself.

It had grown dark now. In the black, torn-up garden plots, vegetables no longer grew. They had by now served a good purpose. Fires crackled noisily, casting weird shadows on the white stucco walls of the house. Claude, all this time, seemed to have learned neither laziness nor lightheartedness, for there he was, as his father had seen him, still earnestly answering the soldiers' demands for second portions.

Instead of being pleased with her son and encouraging him, Marguerite stood in his path, her hands on her hips, glaring down at him.

"Now, then, in you go for supper yourself!" she said, as if furious. "And then to bed. Don't blink your eyes at me! You've had a man's day, so to bed! Oh . . .," she stopped, remembering something. "Make sure you see your father before you go upstairs. He has something to tell you."

At this, Claude blinked indeed, and nearly dropped the soup bowls he was carrying. His mother rescued them and heard him say, "He remembered!" Then he disappeared into the shadow on the way to the house.

A huge army lantern over the lintel bathed the door and the flagstone porch in yellow light. Just as Claude was about to pass through the giant timbers of the door frame, something caught his eye. There, among the heap of muskets, swords and armor lay the splintered remains of the arrow he'd shot that afternoon. He gasped quickly. Before he could turn around and run back the way he had come, he had stepped into the kitchen. His father was not alone and he hid in a nook. At the large oval table with his father sat a half-dozen officers finishing their dinner. Among them was a black-robed priest. As Claude feared, it was the one he least wanted to see.

"How could he have come in without my seeing him?" Claude wondered.

There was soon more than that for Claude to wonder at, for just as the men poured themselves a last glass of wine, and clinked their glasses in the candlelight to toast their own safe arrival, Pere Dupree broke their cheer with an announcement that made Claude's eyes open wider and wider as he heard the words pour out.

"Gentlemen, gentlemen! You toast your arrival 'safely home'? Don't delude yourselves! You surely don't think you're 'safely home,' do you? Why, just this afternoon while I was walking over here to have a conference with our host on a matter concerning his son, I nearly lost my life!" Thus Pere Dupree began, then went on to tell the story of what happened, but with such vivid detail that Claude wondered whether it could be the same incident. If the priest were serious, it would not go well, Claude thought, for his parents loved Pere Dupree.

When the story related the plunge of the arrow, the narrator gestured with his arm. "It came within a foot of making a bulls-eye of my chapeau," he said, illustrating the soaring arc with his arm and almost plunging his finger into Monsieur de la Colombiere's wine glass. One officer turned a smile into a straight face as he caught Claude's eye in the darkened corner.

"What would *you* do, gentlemen?" Pere Dupree asked with a thump of his fist that rattled the empty bottles and glasses on the table.

The men began murmuring about the Huguenots arising again to burn the churches and haunt the clergy until finally the officer whose smile Claude had not quite seen stood up ominously. He was a huge man with a black beard, and his hairy chest showed through his open tunic.

"We're going to Lyons tonight, *mon pere*. The men are anxious to be home at last. But if we see anyone who looks like a guilty one, believe me, *mon pere*, we'll take time out to. . . ." Then he finished with a slow, razor-like gesture across his Adam's apple, glowering at Claude all the while.

"Good!" said Pere Dupree simply. Then, turning to Monsieur de la Colombiere more seriously, he said, rising, "You've made a good decision about Claude, Bertrand. Good night, and God bless you all."

He walked out without looking into the darkness of the nook where Claude still crouched wondering how, if indeed all this were a huge joke for his benefit, Pere Dupree ever knew he was there. But then, the man was a teacher, after all, who had proved more than once that he had eyes in the back of his head!

Up until now those eyes had never caught Claude in mischief, for being tutored at home made it easy for Claude to be a "good boy." Now he wondered more than ever about going to a class in Lyons or anywhere: what kind of boy *was* he? Was he really a "good boy," as his brothers kidded him for being? Or was he really only too well protected? He wondered whether he had ever had a chance to really prove himself.

Anyway, he was glad when the last of the soldiers had slipped out into the night to begin the trek to the Lyons barracks.

When the kitchen was empty, Claude's mother brought in his supper and cleared the table. He watched her in silence.

"Mother," he said finally, "none of them ever said 'thank you,' did they?"

"Oh, well, sometimes people do, Claude," she said cheerfully. "Your father always does. And as long as someone appreciates what we try to do, it's worthwhile." Then, after a pause to look outside where her husband was helping to load the wounded men onto the wagons that he had lent the soldiers for their night ride, she went back to place the dishes in a tub of steaming water. "Besides," she added, "even when your father forgets, God doesn't. The worst days are a kind of joy when we can remember that *He's* grateful that we help those people partly for his sake."

Claude was to remember this night well. Perhaps because of the excitement in the air at the time, he was one day to recall these words of his mother. But for now, he just let them sink into his well of memories that was only beginning to be filled.

For the present, "gratitude" was little more than a new word in his growing vocabulary.

All the fires had been put out. The armor, helmets and sabres were cleared from the door and slung from the saddleries. The family watched the last wagon rumble down the lane with a lantern swinging jauntily from the tailgate.

The yard was a shambles. Only the squash and melons remained in the garden, and they were there only because they hadn't ripened yet. Everything else was gone. Even where the flowers and herbs had been in bloom by the fence, only gnawed stems now stuck up out of the ground, as Madame de la Colombiere was to discover with dismay the next morning.

In the fitful light from the windows, Humbert and Floris were picking up orange peels and bandages and empty wine bottles strewn everywhere over the grass. Claude, with his mother and father, stood silently for a moment on the porch watching the boys. Just as Claude's father looked up at the stars and was remarking what a nice night it was for the army to push on home, a horse whinneyed beyond the fence.

Claude started as if in a dream. "Oh, Papa! They've left a horse behind!" He tore away from his parents, ran to the gate, and ran around behind the fence.

"Papa! Mamma! They've left *two* horses behind. Saddles and everything."

When Claude reappeared at the gate jumping up and down, pointing off into the darkness, he didn't notice his father quietly taking his mother's hand. The horses, whose riders had died crossing the Pyrenees, had been led home riderless and left as gifts to the family.

"Yes, Claude, I know what they look like. One's quite big and the other's small. The big mare's for me."

"Who's the small one for?"

"For you. You've got a little less than a week to become accustomed to his gait. You can start practicing in the morning."

"Oh, Mother, Father, they *did* thank us!" Claude exclaimed rapturously, and Bertrand looked at his small son's serious eyes and at his wife in complete bewilderment.

Claude turned back to the gate. He stood still for a while, taking in the many things that had occurred that day. He looked up at the porch. Now he could easily see that his mother's head was bent down and that she was crying quietly.

3.

Finger of God

NEARLY eight years, had passed since Claude first rode north with his father to begin his schooling in Lyons. How he had longed for Vienne and his family; how exiled he had felt himself to be! Though Pere Dupree and Papa had schooled him in Latin, it had been very difficult to confine his speech to Latin in school. But gradually he spoke as fluently as any and settled into a happy routine with students and masters. Short Christmas and Easter visits to Vienne and summer visits to nearby St. Symphorien, where the family spent the hot weather in the old stone family home, proved to be pleasant breaks in his years of schooling.

On this warm April night in 1658 the stars pierced brightly through the blackness so that one could see the line of carriages winding slowly up the road which led up to the Chateau Villeroi. And in one of the coaches rode Claude and several friends from the college.

The chateau, nestling in an enormous grove of tall pines and poplars, was to be the scene of a ball to which the friends of the King were invited, as well as those families of Lyons connected with the court, who would honor young King Louis XIV.

The party was being given by the Marquis de Villeroi, a friend of the Colombiere family. As the coaches rumbled out of the forest on the long, curving road toward the Chateau Villeroi, they could hear the strains of the violins, flutes and harpsichords pouring forth from the ballroom over the candlelit lawns. At the front door nearly a dozen other carriages were lined up waiting while ladies in their billowy gowns were being helped by footmen up the marble steps. In Claude's carriage the young men were putting on their white gloves. Even in the darkness, however, Andre LaBelle could see that Claude, his best friend, had not gotten into the spirit of things.

"Come now, Claude," he said, "we're not on our way to logic class. Cheer up!"

"Yes," another voice said in a dark corner, "at least manage to show a little nervousness like the rest of us. The way you yawned just then makes you look so frightfully bored — as if this were the sort of thing Trinite students did every night of the year."

The truth was that Claude had been to a good many such affairs in recent years. More than that, he had become quite fond of these parties, as his friends knew only too well. Some friends had of late become a little envious of Claude's reputation for dancing. About his renown for excellence in music, they could afford to be proud; but in the matter of dancing, which made him a favorite partner with the ladies, it was another question altogether.

If Claude actually were bored, it was not with the prospect of the ball, but with the chilly and reserved reaction of his friends at moments like these.

Andre, for his part, knew better. He knew how far Claude was from being bored or blasé about anything. Further, he knew that it was as much Claude's unaffected charm in conversation as his dancing that won him favor with the ladies. If Claude was difficult to understand, it was (Andre had once said) simply because of a depth in Claude that gave him an air of mystery. This, too, was likely to win him friends among the ladies, and lose them among the men. For people could never quite get used to Claude's habit of doing the unexpected.

For example, there was the question of whether he followed

through with the advantage he had gained so easily with the ladies. After so many dances, he said nothing more complimentary than, "How beautifully you dance!" or, "How witty you are!" For this the ladies were grateful enough; but they, too, expected more of him in the way of flattery.

Girls who knew him had given up trying to turn his head, but they still considered him a challenge. They wondered about him. "How can he love to dance so much, and be so good at it, and yet never show any interest in us? He has terribly high ideals," they concluded. "He must be searching for perfection."

And, since quite a few of the young ladies saw perfection reflected in their own mirrors, several smiled warmly at Claude as he and his friends entered the Grande Salle. Some, who were bolder, came up to his group waving their fans, and, under the pretext of welcoming representatives of the college, found themselves gathered around Claude, chattering amiably.

Andre LaBelle was annoyed. "Tonight," he said to a friend, "I am going to employ his strategy. I am going to be sparing in my flattery, aloof in my bearing, and gracious even to the goslings."

"And that will leave you more securely a bachelor than ever, my friend. You miss Claude's charm entirely."

"Well, how do you explain it?"

"I don't. I'm not sure a thing like that can be explained. It is certainly not in his appearance."

That was true. Claude was tall, but so thin as to appear frail. His childhood sickness was still robbing him of vitality. His hair was black, his eyes dark, and his face quite thin. The sparkle of kindness in his eyes was all that prevented him from seeming sad much of the time. If anything could be said to be obviously charming about him, it was not his static features, but the way he focused big eyes on the person he was talking with. This was a kindness he showed even to the "goslings" as Andre called those rather plain people to whom everyone else was merely polite.

As for the way he carried himself, Claude was remarkably

graceful. Whether this was because he loved to dance so much, or the result, no one could tell; but one of Claude's female admirers observed that there was a decided manliness in the way he performed the intricate steps of the minuet. His concern for perfection in this aspect of being a gentleman, she went on to note, had its advantages. It was exactly the sort of agility a man needs to be a good swordsman. But in this, too, Claude had surprised people. He had simply refused to do what was expected of an aspiring man of property — learn to fence. "Why duel over one's honor?" he asked his critics. "That's like children fighting over a worthless toy. And as for defending myself, why make it necessary? If I should be foolish enough ever to gather up so many trinkets that someone should want to kill me to get them, well, then, they can have them without a fight."

Just as the musicians began playing for the first dance and it became time for the gentlemen to choose their partners, the host caught sight of Claude and his friends. The Marquis dramatically raised his arms in welcome, lifted a smile to heaven, and plowed his portly self through clusters of guests like a galleon breasting the waves. With his stubby arm as far up toward Claude's shoulder as he could reach in a showy display of friendship, he had a request to make: would they be so gallant as to sing one song for the guests? Would they show these overly-refined Parisians that the Lyons Jesuits were of the same calibre as those up north that had trained Moliere, Corneille and Descartes?

Yes, they would sing, but please, they asked him, would he not embarrass them by claiming for them the talents of those two great playwrights and that great philosopher, Descartes? They might not be able to compete. He promised, and off they went to the terrace to practice for a moment or two.

These were the days when to be an aristocrat in France was to be thoroughly involved with the arts. Many, like the Marquis, felt the need to compete for favor with the King by being a patron (as he was) of French artists. Only a month previous, when an envoy of the court visited Lyons, the Marquis saw to it that the college put on a play as entertainment, Thus it was, by inspiring such splendor, that King Louis was becoming known as *le Roi Soleil*, the "Sun King," even at an early age.

At the end of the minuet, Claude and seven other young men delighted the guests with a motet by Palestrina. Though at times each voice sang a different part from all the rest, each part sounded like a melody all its own, yet blending sweetly with all the others. When they finished, the ballroom was so filled with applause and calls of "Encore!" "Bravo!" that they sang two more songs. Claude was clearly enjoying himself now. Nothing on earth pleased him as much as what he was doing at that moment.

Andre's bewilderment can be imagined, then, when the two young men encountered two of Claude's admirers and Claude excused himself. "I'm very sorry," he said, "but I find I must go home early."

Characteristically, however, he stayed long enough talking to Mlle. Charpentier and her sister until two other friends came to ask the girls to dance. Andre was the more vexed at seeing what he considered the two fairest young ladies in Lyons walking off on someone else's arm.

"Well!" he said in exasperation, following Claude to the door, "pardon me for wasting your time with the most promising friend of our college years."

"She seems a very lovely person, Andre."

"Of course she is, but that is not what I mean."

"Oh?"

"Oh, indeed! Do you recall who her father is?"

"Monsieur Charpentier, no doubt," said Claude, smiling.

"Monsieur Charpentier, the wealthiest and most influential judge in southern France, if you please."

"It's a pity a man couldn't marry him!"

"Don't be funny, Claude. A man in your position can't afford to be so nonchalant about his future friends."

"My position?"

"Why, of course! A lawyer is to his judges as a captain is to his generals. Any fool knows that."

"Oh, so it's all arranged for me to become a lawyer!"

They had reached the porch outside by now, and were waiting for the next carriage to town. Andre answered Claude's last remarks by looking him intently in the face.

"Why, of course you're going to be a lawyer. Everyone's known that for years!"

"I see!" said Claude. He wasn't looking at Andre, but out into the night. He felt like changing the subject. With a barely perceptible grin, he said, "It's a wonderful night, Andre!"

"For going to bed? You're a little crazy, I think, Claude."

"For not staying longer here? Come now, Andre, you sound like someone who'd never seen the end of a dance before."

"No, I'm not thinking of the dance. Even I'd be crazy not to stay if dancing were all there were to a night like this."

"Ah, so it's the girls — that's what I'm crazy not to notice."

"Yes," Andre replied almost angrily, "and how they fawn all over you."

A coach was rumbling up on the crunchy gravel to the steps. Claude clipped on his cape and stepped inside.

He picked up Andre's last words. "And for not noticing what a fascinating evening it would be if I were to remain and do what's expected of me?"

"Yes, confound it!"

"I'll tell you a secret, Andre. I do notice. I do!"

Andre felt the coach start to move, and let go the door handle. "Well, why don't you stay, then?" He found himself having to yell, "Why don't you stay?"

But it was too late for an answer. Claude just waved, smiling more mysteriously than ever as the carriage disappeared into the night.

Andre remained till early in the morning, but his joviality was disturbed. Nothing in this thinking prepared him to explain these quirks in Claude.

"He likes the girls and yet he leaves them." Unable to solve the riddle, Andre did his best to forget it.

The next morning broke warm and sunny, with just a hint of gray after the showers in the hills. Because it was Sunday the boys were allowed to sleep late; until five-thirty, that is, a half-hour later than on class days. From the University Church the spire rose up like an arrow to catch the morning sunlight on its tip. Before the whole spire was aglow, the bells pealed out over the city to wake silk-weavers and shopkeepers as well as students and bring them to six o'clock Mass.

This was to be Pere Papon's farewell to Lyons. After teaching philosophy at Trinite for six years, he had gotten a new "status" from his Provincial. On Monday he was to leave for Avignon, down river, where he would take up his new life as Master of Novices at the Jesuit novitiate.

One thing Claude would always remember about his college years was the sermon Pere Papon gave that Sunday. It was on a subject rather well known to all of France in those times — the missions in North America. So well was the story known, in fact, that no sooner had Pere Papon announced his subject than Andre nodded his head and began snoring softly in his pew. Claude, sitting next to him, squinted his eyes, bit his lips, and gave Andre such a dislodging with his knee that Andre, thinking it was time for the *Credo*, jumped to his feet before Claude could pull him down. Several of the boys snickered in the seat behind, but it all happened so quickly that Claude missed little of the sermon.

Tired as he was, Claude wanted to listen as carefully as he could, because, among other reasons, Pere Papon was his spiritual director in the Sodality. Thus Claude was listening to the one man in the world who knew him best, and who happened to be, in a different way from Andre, his best friend.

"Who has not heard again and again of Isaac Jogues?" Pere Papon asked in the rhetorical style of Cicero, so much studied and admired in academic circles since the Renaissance. "Who has not thrilled from his earliest days to the heroic fortitude of Jean de Brebeuf? Who can wander up and down our streets complacently, knowing there are Frenchmen like ourselves facing death hourly, who walked yesterday where we walk today?"

Claude loved his old, Roman style of speaking; but there was always a point where he ceased hearing only sentences and words, and when ideas began coming through the rolling sounds.

"Many are the lanes in France where we have walked after Pere Jogues; but who of us will run with him up the hill on the shore of the Mohawk River in New France? Picture ourselves dashing up with him among his Huron converts between two lines of Iroquois savages who wait to strike us with their sticks and clubs! Who of us will 'run the gauntlet' for our Lord?"

Andre, who had fallen asleep again, mumbled something unintelligible. No one dared wake him now.

"Yet those martyrs grew up in France, wearing lace ruffles and powdered wigs to royal dances. They have drunk the finest wines in the most civilized cities in the world. Now where are they? They have wintered in the forest, starved in savage huts; they have drunk melted snow and bent their finely trained minds to learning the Huron tongue."

This was just the way old Cicero would have addressed the Roman Senate. And nobody should know this better than Pere Papon who had taught Cicero's Latin to Claude and his class. Yet here was Andre still fast asleep beside him, totally unaroused. Surely, Claude thought, something must be wrong with a speaking style that couldn't keep a young man awake on such a subject — even a young man who had spent much of the night dancing. Somehow, Claude had to admit to himself, Pere Papon's veneration for the Ancients led him to sound unnatural, even insincere. Though nothing could be further from the truth in this brave priest's case, Claude had to agree with what Andre had said once — that Pere Papon seemed to be as interested in sounding properly like his Roman master as in telling the unvarnished truth about the martyrs. How unfortunate that such a sincere man could even seem to be artificial! Claude couldn't help thinking how *he* would tell the martyrs' story if *he* were in the pulpit.

Just then, in the midst of these distractions, Claude heard Pere Papon reach the climax of his sermon. "I seem to hear you say, my friends, that this is not for me. You think of Pere Brebeuf's death and wonder, 'What had this martyr to teach me?' There he is, my friends. Picture him standing on the torturers' platform. Even the savages admire him! Even the Iroquois must discover the limits of his endurance, and then drink his blood to inherit his bravery. Watch them approach with fiery eyes and string around his neck six red-hot hatchet heads. See the water boiling nearby which they will pour on him in derision of the baptism they have seen the blackrobe perform. Yes, my brothers, but watch even more carefully Pere Brebeuf himself. See there, how even as the savages are slicing off his flesh with their crude flint-knives, he is praying for them! Listen to him encourage his converts in their native tongue, he who knows all the languages of Europe! Hear the words come through his face streaming with blood, from where they have cut off his nose and lips!"

"Even the savages wonder what motives a man must have to endure such torment. Now they perform the last rite in their test of bravery. They scalp our countryman and tear out his heart with their fingers. They will drink the blood of this man's heart thinking it will make them brave, too!"

"The heart," thought Claude, "How little they understood the heart — and yet how well."

"Most of you will never leave France," Pere Papon went on. "May I ask you, just the same, to think of what these martyrs' lives mean to you? Martyr means witness, as you know. Here are two questions, then: first, what are these men giving witness to so far from home? Is it not to the reality of God's grace and to its power to move the hearts of savages, when men have failed? And second: is there no way in which we too can be martyrs, or witnesses, here in France?"

For the first time during the sermon, Pere Papon smiled broadly. "But do not expect me to answer all my questions. I simply do not know the answers. You do, though! Only you can tell exactly how you are called to be a witness. God bless you all!"

To everyone's surprise, Andre was wide-awake and standing for the *Credo* before anyone else. He turned to Claude and whispered, "The smile in his voice woke me."

One day Claude would profit from Andre's slumber. For the rest of Mass, however, he was distracted by something else. Pere Papon was a happy man. In fact all the Jesuits he had come to know were uncommonly happy and friendly. Somehow even Jean de Brebeuf and Isaac Jogues impressed him as having been happy, or at least as having known exactly what they were doing and why, if that were so different from happiness.

Suddenly Claude realized what he would do. It was as simple and as natural as going home for the holidays. He would see Pere Papon about becoming a Jesuit. And he would see him right after Mass.

Claude caught a glimpse of Andre yawning as they genuflected for the last Gospel and thought, "If he only knew!"

Minutes later Claude and Pere Papon were talking as they strolled along the paths under the college elms. How easy to bring up this subject! Claude had once imagined it an agony, and here he was with a hundred ways to begin. He chose the sermon and Pere Papon's unanswered question.

"Of course the reason is that they loved God," Claude heard him say as they walked slowly along the gravel paths of the college. "That's why they took the vows as Jesuits. But that doesn't mean at all that you should think of taking vows, too, just because you love God as well. It's very generous of you to offer your life to our Lord this way, but after all, Claude, I don't want you to think that some of these wonderful laymen here in town love God less because they wear a more colorful coat than we do. Everybody's called to love," Pere Papon shrugged his shoulders doubtfully. "I'm not even ready to say that a person couldn't love more in riding boots and doublet than some of us in black!"

Was the good father serious? This wasn't at all what Claude had expected. Was the man teasing him? Playing hard to get? Claude had always been certain that when a young man presented himself to a religious order he would be welcomed, provided he was in good health and was a good student. Everyone had heard that it was "better to be a good layman than a bad priest," but was this really the question in Pere Papon's mind? Was Claude a "good boy" after all, but not really good enough? Had Claude's record at *la Trinite* been good enough to recommend him for a lawyer's firm or for a bank, but lacking in something necessary to be a Jesuit? Claude's vanity suffered a blow at this turn of the conversation.

"What are you getting at, *mon pere*?" Claude asked. "Is it that I am not good enough to be a Jesuit? Is that it? Please don't be afraid to tell me."

"Ha, ha! No, my boy, it's not that at all! If anything, perhaps you are too good. The Lord was a friend of sinners and had them for disciples. And we're no holier than our Lord, as our friends are likely to remind us at any time. No, and I'm not suggesting either that you go out and get more worldly 'experience.' "

Pere Papon laughed at the drift the conversation was now taking. "No, not that. You're already enough of a shiner to be a good disciple. But I do suggest, Claude, that you don't really know very much about the Society you want to join. Oh, not that you don't know all the stories of the saints. You know them well enough. But I'd no more encourage you to become a Jesuit knowing only Jean de Brebeuf or Isaac Jogues, than I'd encourage an Iroquois to become a Frenchman knowing only King Louis XIV. The poor savage might find his niche in France a little humbler than he'd expected."

"But, *mon pere*, I do know more about the Society than that. I do know you and the life the fathers lead as teachers."

Pere Papon caught the inference and laughed. "Ha, ha! Thank you for putting me in my niche! Yes, you know the top *and* the bottom, don't you? But seriously, Claude, do you really know me? You see me in the classroom, talk to me in the confessional, serve my Mass sometimes, and have an occasional walk with me in the garden here. Just think, though — if a man entered marriage with as little knowledge of how to succeed in *that* vocation as he would get from watching his father going over his papers in the evenings before the fireplace, I'd say he would be in for a few surprises, wouldn't you, Claude?"

"I suppose so, *mon pere.*"

"Let me tell you something, then. Let me tell you about the hours of our life that you've never seen."

As Claude listened to the long tale of the trials of the novitiate, and of the years of study, fourteen altogether, his face became sad. For Pere Papon was not entirely joking about Claude's not being "experienced" enough to be a good disciple. Truly, he was not a sinner like Magdalene or the good thief. Nevertheless, Claude was far enough from being a "goody-goody" to have enjoyed his social life immensely. So he told Pere Papon how he loved the parties and the dances at the Duke's chateau. He told him about never missing a concert in the eight years he had lived in Lyons, and how he went so often to the theater that he knew many of the parts by heart.

Now all this was to go! As he heard Pere Papon resume the tale of being a Jesuit scholastic, of teaching maybe in some remote village, he realized that even so small a liberty as wandering around town from one restaurant to another in search of friends was going to be canceled out by the vows of both poverty *and* obedience. What would it be like not to be able to go to dances, even if he went only for the liberty of leaving them?

He could go on studying.

"And even then, after all this," Pere Papon concluded, "after all this training, you might never use it again in your life. After all the philosophy and theology and literature, you might be sent to some unadventurous mission and have to teach the catechism to children in a native dialect. Mind you, unadventurous! That's perhaps the most difficult awakening of all. To realize that you may be sent, without your wanting it in the least, to a land you would never have cared to *hear* about, to do a job you were never really trained for; and remember this, Claude, not just for a few years, as may be true here in France, but for the rest of your life! For many of us, Claude, there are never any vacations, never any visits home."

The last remark was designed to touch Claude in his most sensitive nerve. It did, and he remained silent for several minutes. Then, turning to his confessor he said, "*Mon pere*, I have the greatest aversion for the life you describe."

Pere Papon looked long at Claude. Then he looked away down the path toward the hills. "One does have to know oneself, and a bit about the Society to make a statement like that."

Claude waited.

"And yet you would like to become a Jesuit?"

"Yes, *mon pere*."

"Claude. . . ." Pere Papon turned his gaze away from the southern horizon where thunderheads had gathered and looked into the young man's somber face. "I think the finger of God is here."

4.

"Bright and Burning"

At Avignon
August, 1661

My dear brother Floris,

In speaking of the death of our mother, what can be said? In your message to me, you said it all, Floris. Especially did I feel the comment Humbert made in his wise, brotherly way, that "she was that perfect friend, a mother who kept all doors open within her family so that one or all could sit down and talk, coming away richer, feeling befriended."

How true of little Mere Marguerite! She gave me such confidence when I had her that I feel little pain now, only to look forward to seeing her when my years are through.

Pere Papon offered Mass for her and we say the Rosary and her favorite Litany of Loreto each evening.

I don't believe you could have known how much influence she had in persuading Papa to consent to my vocation. In my mind, the matter was settled when I talked with Pere Papon before he left Lyons. I think Mother knew I couldn't change, in spite of my fear and aversion to the deadly routine and anonymity of life in an order. She knew I must face this myself.

But Father! He was convinced that I "did not know what I wanted; that I thought I would be a hero; I should allow him to use his influence to obtain a nice bishopric or an abbey for me!"

So went his discourse in his deep concern for his "impractical" son.

Poor Mother! But then my application was accepted and I was ready to leave St. Symphorien. Our dear old home! If we do not feel that this was our "heaven on earth" it will not have been Mother's fault.

Floris, you must know that our father is quite a hero to me. Once we had set out, he and I, on the journey to Avignon, he seemed to have turned his back upon resistance and set his mind to encouragement for me. How difficult this was for him only he would know.

Jean LaGaste waited for us at Condrieu. Mme. LaGaste served us cool buttermilk and biscuits before we continued to Montelimar that night. Father bought some little red Morocco leather slippers for Mother. Did he take any of the nougat home to you? It was delicious, but we had to persuade Jean to try it — it looked so much like soap!

From the banks of the turbulent lower Rhone the Alps soar to unimagined heights. You must someday see this grandeur. How small we felt! I wondered how one made the choice, amid such surroundings, between feeling insignificant and of aspiring to magnificent deeds.

Then we came to Avignon. Here the river is a little more calm. The city is old, so old — the Avenio of the Romans, actually, and elm-shaded and vine-covered, and guarded everywhere by rising towers. Bells in the many bell towers broadcast dissonant concerts each day.

Pere Papon's words of greeting warmed me and reassured Papa, who returned home next morning, pleading business affairs.

The winter mistral still plagues me with my old trouble in breathing. But we are comfortable here, if you remember how different community life is.

Where else, for example, would you be likely to find your

brother, Claude, busy at his duties of scrubbing beets and leeks or of cultivating carrots and cabbage or of passing soup and bread to the diners in the refectory? I do not dislike these tasks ordinarily, but sweeping and weeding are so tiring! What would I not do sometimes for a chance to go and hide — or to plead illness — but I remember the knowledge of myself which I brought here with me and how I resolved to do what was required even if it were repugnant to me.

Let me tell you about a certain boy named Auguste. Next time you eat soup, Floris, recall Auguste, who enjoys it so. He enjoys the warm steam, the rich liquid, the sipping and the sucking and the smacking. Auguste reaches for another spoonful with a musical "whack" against his pottery bowl. He chews and smacks his lips over the soup and crouton. And the end of the bowl is a delight for scooping and scraping. Floris, this was a spectacle the first time, amusing the second, an event to dread the fifth time, and since then, an unbelievable horror! What does one do? Nothing; at least, nothing that others can see. One sits quietly, eats calmly the soup which seems about to fly off one's spoon at these shocking sounds. This daily trial is offered, in all humility, for some great or little cause. Did I hear you say that you plan to come into the Order? Welcome, little brother!

One day you may meet a young man as conscientious as Phillipe. No one can have any hidden faults when he's about! Phillipe has taken to keeping me informed. Yesterday he told me that Pierre has a sack of candy hidden in his clothes closet. Today, Isaac was caught climbing the old olive tree to look over the wall toward the river. Isaac loves the river and this is his first year here. Poor Phillipe hasn't caught his own fault yet. But how it bothers me to hear all these tales when I have so long been impatient with such tittle-tattle!

Pere Papon soon put me in my place when I asked to talk it over with him. He asked, "Did you think when you came here you would associate only with people you felt inclined to help? A few purist Jansenists to convert, perhaps, or some sick people all neatly put up in hospitals; and for the rest, a crowd of stylish, well-fed members of *a congregation? Is that what St. Francis Xavier was looking for? Is this what Father Francis de Sales expected?"*

I knew there would be no buffer between me and these everyday troubles. My problem is not to persuade a theoretical Jansenist nor to convert a province in Cathay, but to overcome Claude de la Colombiere day by day. I must try to see the soul and mind in my friends, not to see or hear their all too human traits. Please believe me, Floris, this is a daily task worthy of a stronger will than mine!

How I wish you had been with us when His Majesty, King Louis XIV, visited Pope Alexander right here in Avignon. The visit was scarcely announced when the halls at the Palace de La Motte seemed to shimmer in the glow of all the excitement. We had many tasks to perform: polishing windows and brasswork, waxing floors, clipping hedges and weeding gardens. Who could know? King Louis himself might come to this very house; any one of us might see him. (Yes, he came, and we all saw him.)

If our own Duc de Villeroi were coming I thought I might be presented to the King myself, though I took care not to say this.

It was during Holy Week that we were most drawn into ceremonies. On Holy Thursday the King knelt down and washed the feet of twelve poor men, an astounding spectacle for students. Even with their calloused, knobby feet, these men were as angels compared with the victims of the "King's Evil," upon whom he later put his hand so calmly, not seeming to notice the cracked, raw skin and the ugly neck sores of this unpleasant disease which is widely thought to be healed by the touch of a king's hand.

Our school was represented at the Easter reception for King Louis by Pere Papon, who chose me to accompany him. He briefed me as we hurried down the lane in the moonlight. We went to the reception hall to await the arrival of the King and his mother and their entourage. It was splendid! Father's friend, the Duc de Villeroi, presented me to many people. Floris, a very strange man seemed to watch me. Monsieur Jean Baptiste Colbert is a close advisor to the King. It may be his mobile face and extremely intelligent eyes that haunt me.

King Louis had lost some of that youthful exaltation that Andre and I saw in him that time in Lyons, but there is a reserve and dignity now which seems to suit a king. The rumors that come to us seem to hint that he and the Pope have been at odds for a couple of years and have made an uncertain peace with each other. We ordinary people are not alone in our problems, Floris.

You speak quite seriously of coming into the Order. Think well, little brother. You are indeed making a fine record at Lyons, but there is a vast difference. If you do decide, I will be the first to rejoice.

> *With love,*
> *Claude*

In the years following, many letters kept the brothers informed about each other. Humbert was a successful businessman by now. Floris was increasingly certain he would follow after Claude, while Marguerite and tiny Joseph, born after Claude left home, were convinced even in their childhood that they, too, would be religious.

Claude taught rhetoric and then the humanities to younger students. The city of Avignon was seldom aware of this group of students, so quiet and unobtrusive were their ways; but fathers and relatives often visited them, bringing news of Paris. Claude heard that his father's acquaintance, who had observed him at the reception for the King was now minister of finance and that King Louis was indeed becoming a strong, admirable ruler. Since disagreement was still evident at times between certain factions in the government (upon the issue of whether the Pope would guide the Church in France or whether the King would have the decisive voice in the French Church), Avignon citizens were torn between a sense of allegiance to the Papacy and to the French King. Two political factions in the ancient city often fought each other, not only in speeches and by social snubs and political rivalries, but also in street fights. Youthful partisans, having no means of potent action, resorted to rock-throwing and name-calling toward each other, which often proved dangerous to pedestrians, particularly to the nonpartisan young seminarians strolling for the air.

A letter in 1666 to Humbert told of Claude's being drawn into this state of affairs indirectly, chiefly because of his special ability in oration.

At Avignon
June 5, 1666

My dear brother Humbert,

If my hand is a little unsteady and the writing not as clear as usual, please forgive it. Your brother has a difficult task awaiting him this evening, one which is taking much of his time and attention. How this came about, I can only guess, though there seems to be a solution here to the puzzle of why I have been assigned so many sermons.

Pere Chabrand called me to his office one day a few weeks ago. I'll try to quote him: "My son, I have been following your progress carefully, especially in the development of sermons and orations you have prepared and delivered. They show increasing thought and wit, particularly your recent 'Panegyric to Panegyrists.' How well you handled the political feelings of the crowd here at Avignon and yet even in giving advice, did not offend!

"We have been planning our celebration in honor of the canonization of Blessed Francis de Sales in May and June. Though we have many priests and bishops skilled in oratory, with fine forensic ability, each one who has been suggested has at one time or another spoken out either in favor of Pope Alexander VII or of King Louis XIV. Since this will be a mixed crowd at the ceremonies, we need a fresh voice, one which has as yet offended no group.

"You have been chosen."

Humbert, this, in brief, is the cause of my preoccupation these past weeks when my letters to the family have been short; and the

*cause also, I fear, of my present writing at greater length. For I am
prepared, and now I escape for a while to my family.*

*You will be wise, you must know, to pray that I shall not feel
vainglory if I please my superiors, even as I pray that I may speak in a
way that offends none. However, success will soothe dear Pere Papon,
especially after the decline in my marks last year.*

*Do you remember that little book Father had at home which we
used to look at so often? It had been sent to us from the Visitandine
Monastery founded by Blessed Francis de Sales and Jane de Chantal.
In our childhood we thought the pictures most important, especially
the one over which we whispered — and even carried to Father Francis
at our parish church for explanation — a heart, surrounded by
flames, which Mother told us was the Blessed Francis' coat of arms.*

This same device, inscribed, Lucens et Ardens *is represented in
the decorations in the square where I shall give my sermon. The subject
I have chosen? That old enigma of Samson's, "Out of the strong came
forth sweetness." This theme should not be found offensive — or I shall
hope that it will not. Following the ceremonies the wooden heart and
the paper angels, the flowers and ferns, will all be set ablaze. Will the
spectacle be more impressive than my sermon? That shall be as God
wills.*

*I should soon be assigned to other studies away from Avignon;
where, I do not know.*

*Give my love to Marguerite and Joseph, reminding them to pray
for me.*

> *With love,*
> *Claude*

Claude folded the letter and lighted a candle. He melted the
sealing wax on the fold and sealed it with the Colombiere seal. He
looked around the spotless room and snuffed out the flame. The letter
went onto the hall shelf to be picked up by the next messenger going

up the river. Claude went out into the evening twilight carrying his hat.

He turned to a lane beside a hedge, above which arose a wooded knoll. What was this vague feeling of recognition which came to him in the spring evening? Suddenly, he chuckled. He could almost see the excited little boys at the top of distant Salamont and a priest strolling at the foot beside a hedge. Involuntarily his own hand went to his hat as though to make certain it was still there.

A crowd milled around in the square, talking. Groups stood here and there to admire the decorations, the lovely flower-decked heart. A feeling of recognition came again to Claude. Surely it must be an echo of his earlier knowledge of this device: But was it really? It almost seemed that this would not be the end of his knowledge of this emblem — this heart — *Lucens et Ardens.* It was a feeling difficult to shake off.

A few weeks after this event Claude was handed a letter enclosed in the very finest vellum. A most important seal closed the fold. How should such a packet come to the hands of a young Jesuit? Claude found it to be from that "strange man," Monsieur Colbert, the finance minister to Louis XIV. He had, it seemed, heard of Claude's recent sermons and would like to talk with Claude on a "matter of some importance."

This amounted, almost, to a royal command!

5.

"Failure"

CLAUDE reached out to clutch the handgrip on the side of the small, roughly pitching coach. At the same time he pulled the leather window curtain back and caught his first glimpse of a street lamp lighting up its own small area of the cobbled street. The coachman could be heard shouting wordy and impatient instructions at the snorting horses and slapping the reins on their backs.

Claude had heard about the paving of streets and the lighting of the roads which Jean Baptiste Colbert had provided for Paris and thought to himself, "This energetic man's letter to me rests here in my own suitcase. Hm-m-m! What do you suppose he can possibly want with me?"

At least these cobbles must make for better wheeling than the mud which folks said had prevailed until lately, though they were rougher than the journey by canalboat down the Seine River. Claude had arrived at the Paris docks just at sunset on this October evening. After winding through narrow Paris streets all through the dimming twilight, the coach should bring him at any moment to the Rue St. Jacques and the gate of the Jesuit College of Clermont.

Ha! This must be it! With another sway and lurch, the coach stopped, though the horses still stamped and pawed at the cobblestones.

Claude took up his small suitcase while the driver handed down the larger grip to the college porter. Collecting his fee, the coachman drove off with a clatter.

Claude and the old porter walked to the entrance hall and stopped before the huge fireplace and warm fire, where Claude shook off some of the October chill from his bones. A few introductions and greetings and some warm supper were a prelude to his greatest need — a good night's sleep.

Before sunrise the hurry and purposefulness of early morning in a large institution dazed him. The thought came to him that he might never be able to cope with all of it. Not only the theological students and teachers arose at four-thirty ready for the start of a day, but nearly four hundred and fifty boarders and over a thousand day students began work at five o'clock. One professor remarked of Clermont, "A small kingdom in itself!"

Providentially, Claude was able to talk with Pere de Champs, the rector of the college. "Your record in Avignon was excellent, Claude. Not only your studies but your ability as a speaker have been your recommendation to Clermont. Your general level of culture and your poise in dealing with people were also considered.

"But one question: have you any word about a Monsieur Colbert?" he asked with a quizzical look.

"Yes, Father de Champs. I have a letter here. It puzzled me to receive it. I don't know what it concerns."

"You have a relative or a family friend, the Duc de Villeroi?"

"He is a friend of my father's family."

"Ah, yes! Well, Claude, you may have tomorrow to visit some of the classes and see what goes on here. On Monday you will be on schedule. I will make the appointment for you to see Monsieur Colbert."

"Well," thought Claude, "Father de Champs is certainly not free with his information."

As Father de Champs had inferred, appointment to Clermont did not come easily. The curriculum demanded the finest minds available, and only those seminarians having outstanding talents or abilities were accepted.

The time soon came when he was to see Monsieur Colbert. It was an encounter which he had dreaded. It took place in Colbert's handsome library. Looking over at the grim countenance dominated by the sharp eyes, Claude felt that he was ready for almost anything. He listened to the flat, almost toneless voice.

"Well, well! So, Claude de la Colombiere, we meet again! You are the young man who is to teach my sons. You must remember I do not like these Jesuits; but — they have the best school in Paris and I want my sons thoroughly prepared to take government positions. Teach them well!" Not a wasted word, no time given to graciousness, not even an effort toward politeness.

Claude was not surprised to hear the antagonism toward the Jesuits. It was not fashionable to be a Jesuit nor to cling to traditional Catholic beliefs. Jansenism had become the most popular of the many sects demonstrating, as their adherents thought, freedom of thought, independence from tradition.

Whatever Claude felt toward this pompous, domineering man he kept to himself, trying to stir up more charity in his thoughts. He knew that M. Colbert was valued by the King for his abilities. Besides seeing that the streets of Paris were cleaned and well lighted, Colbert had organized the East India Company which was setting up colonies in New France. He had brought great wealth to France through the trade in furs and was called the "Merchant Prince."

"I hope you understand," the man dared Claude, "that I don't bother with religions observances except when the King orders a royal ceremony."

"You doubtless attend Sunday Mass," hazarded Claude.

"Of course not! Could I run businesses in France and in New France, halfway around the world, as well as provide so well for my family if I ran to church all the time? There are seven days to the week, you know." His tone continued scathing.

"Ah, yes, M. Colbert! And there would be only six except the Lord gave us one on which to rest and recollect our lives."

"I know, too," Colbert went on, ignoring this statement, "that I am entitled to choose for myself. Since even *you* will admit that not all will be saved, and since I have no assurance of *my* salvation, it is my right to make as much of this world mine as I possibly can while I am here!"

Claude knew he must not offend this man, for the sake of the Order. His mild reply could not have been challenged. "M. Colbert, as you say, you have no assurance of salvation. But if you could receive the Blessed Sacrament often, you would be surprised at the strength and help you would be given," and Claude smiled in a friendly, disarming way. M. Colbert added one more reason for liking and trusting this young man.

The Colbert family naturally enjoyed a position of confidence in the government of Louis XIV. With the King they felt that the State should dominate the Church and that the Pontiff should be a mere figurehead, if, indeed he should have any place at all within the realm of France. The rift between Louis and the Pope was widely known and much debated. But this breach between the political and ecclesiastical powers of France did not alter the intention of M. Colbert to maintain a coolly practical design when he trusted his handsome elder son, Jean Baptiste, the Marquis de Siegnelay, to the Jesuits for his training.

Jean Baptiste, sixteen, and his brother Nicholas, thirteen, were to be molded by the finest teachers in Europe — in the hope that their future would be enhanced by superior tutelage, and more particularly by Claude de la Colombiere, whose fame for superlative homilies and incisive wit was unquestioned. He would tutor Jean in the humanities and Nicholas in grammar. Though most of these special students at Clermont were placed in classrooms for five or six pupils, the Colbert boys had a room reserved to them alone in their work with Claude at the college.

There were times when Claude's assignment took him to the

Colbert's home for assistance with their studies. His work with them wasn't limited to books and recitations, but expanded to attention to the whole character. He appeared frequently with Jean and Nicholas, playing tennis with them on the lawn and participating with them in riding, hunting and fencing, always guiding them in sportsmanship and courtly manners. He often had tea or chocolate with the family and became a frequent guest at their larger gatherings.

Pere de Champs watched this activity closely. Claude was urged to accept invitations of which many other seminarians could only dream. He attended informal receptions at the palace and often heard Mass in the new chapel at Versailles, where he listened to the music of the newly composed *Dies Irae* by Lully. Claude's delight with music increased with each year. Frescobaldi's music was played for his enjoyment on harpsichords in many of the homes he visited. Claude seemed the ideal young Jesuit. Relations between the Merchant Prince and the College continued to run smoothly.

Pere de Champs questioned Claude one day, "Claude, our young Colbert friends are doing well, are they not?"

"Very well, Father, they are excellent students." Claude paused and waited.

"In your estimation, are they inclined to think as their father does in matters of religion? As you know, we have the greatest desire to see harmony restored between the monarchy and the Holy See. Our success with the Colbert sons might help to reconcile some of the disunity by winning M. Colbert's good will, and perhaps result in a like softening of King Louis' feelings."

"Father, I am happy to tell you that the boys are being taught each subject with a good, sound background of philosophy. During one of our recent games, Nicholas reminded Jean that they had agreed to receive Holy Communion together on Pentecost. When Jean replied that he had not forgotten, Nicholas remarked, 'I wish we could get Father to come with us, but he always says that he may the next time.'

" 'Well,' Jean answered, the time will come when he won't be quite so busy.' I don't really believe he's as indifferent as some of the people say. Oh, I've heard some of the fellows at school talk. But he really is busy. He'll be all right!"

"It seems they know of their father's boast that he can make out without the Church but they assure me they constantly pray he will be given the grace to change."

"Then they, at least, don't believe in a rationed, unchangeable store of grace," Pere de Champs chuckled. "Jean quite covered himself with glory last July when he defended his thesis before the Court and Parliament. His structure and his philosophy were equally strong. You did a remarkable piece of work in coaching him on that. It may be by way of reflection, but the glory is there for you, also."

Claude laughed, but hastened to remind Pere de Champs that soon Jean would repeat his performance in sustaining his thesis for this year against one of their own professors, in his father's presence. "And," finished Claude, "he is at least as well prepared as last year."

"Excellent, Claude. If we can only give these sons of their father such a sound background that they will never be tempted to the father's spiritual weakness!"

This sound background of which Pere de Champs spoke would be displayed publicly by each student in the defense of his own thesis as he gained in skill and experience. Jean was prepared and now must show his skill in the presence of his father, his teachers and the student body.

It came about that Jean carried off such a triumph that his father had notes of congratulation from near and far, even from Rome. He was quite exultant over the treatment the hitherto scorned Jesuits were according to his sons.

Claude's involvement with this family was clearly taking much of his time. It happened that the ornately enameled family carriage drew up to the college gate more and more often. Claude began to take this as a courtesy due him. He sometimes had little qualms of conscience, but was able to remind himself that he had not asked for this assignment; he was doing his duty as he had been told. A little point bothered him still, though, like a hornet buzzing about in front of his nose. It was a question of why he had offered his life to the Church. His mind seemed to insist that luxurious carriages and musicals were not likely means to a saintly crown.

Yet he was undeniably drawn to the friends he could make here. The Colberts' new country home was still being landscaped. Gardeners planted shrubs and flowers while masons built walls and bridges, waterfalls and arches, until a fairyland setting had evolved. Candles and lanterns lighted up these scenes for parties attended by princes and dukes who, with their ladies, were bejeweled and costumed in rich silks and laces. Food was imported from many parts of the known world to intrigue the appetites of these critical guests. And these magnificent people were amusing. They talked of New France and of shipping, and of literature, music and philosophy, all of which Claude found stimulating.

Such parties! And, in the same city, such fear and misery! These were the days of brilliance and beauty contrasted with doubt and recklessness. Were there not secret societies which practiced the fearful Black Mass and the worship of Satan? And were there not clever people like the Marchioness de Brinvilliers who slyly practiced with poisons on the poor patients in the charity hospitals, gaining skill which she would use in her political intrigues against enemies? All of these were to be met in Paris. And the contrasts harried a conscience such as Claude's.

One of Claude's friends, Isaac Germaine, walking with him one day, asked, "You, Claude, are invited to some of the most fashionable homes in Paris. Don't you ever feel tempted to leave the Jesuit life?"

"Isaac, let me tell you a secret. I do enjoy this magnificence. When I ride in that enameled carriage drawn by white horses, I feel as important as King Louis himself!"

"Ah! The Sun-King! There is one who knows how to be a King! What a leader he is!"

"Yes, Isaac, but there is a sad picture, too. Have you visited the prisons yet? Or the Hotel Dieu for charity patients? Or the miserable homes in the Porte-St. Marin? This is another side of our glorious Paris. Thank God I have seen both sides!

"Isaac, I visited this morning with a poor, sick man who lay on moldy straw on the floor. He's one of the people who is not able to move to a cleaner home where he will have sunshine and fresh air. He is trapped by age and poverty."

As the young men walked along the narrow street they heard a swish overhead. The contents of a pot of garbage landed at the feet of the students, only just missing their clothes. This kind of disposal was a common practice in the narrow streets.

"Colbert had better hurry over to this street!" remarked Isaac with a nervous laugh, while he and Claude examined their suits.

One foggy, dark morning during the following week, Claude found himself trudging down the middle of one of these alleys on a mission of mercy.

A boy with a twisted leg sat on a doorstep munching a dry bun and regarding Claude with some interest and suspicion.

Claude said, "How's the breakfast, young fellow? Can you tell me where Jules Darnel lives?"

"Go around the alley and up three flights of stairs. But he won't like to see you, Father; he won't let you in."

"Thank you, boy; we'll soon see, won't we?" and Claude laughed, despite the boy's warning.

Claude ascended the stairs humming, "Regina Coeli" (Queen of Heaven), one of his favorite hymns. At the top of the flights he was still singing, "Laetare, O Maria!" He stopped at a doorway. A trembling voice came through the door opening, "Who is that? Who is there?"

"Jules Darnel? I am Claude de la Colombiere. I have come to talk to you."

Claude looked down at the thin man lying on a cot. A patched, dirty blanket covered him. On the table stood a bowl which had yesterday probably been filled with soup brought by a pitying but forgetful neighbor.

"You look like a priest. If you are, I won't talk to you!" the man said as he pulled the blanket over his head.

Claude was not yet a priest, but he said nothing, waiting and praying for a chance to reach this lonely soul.

After a few minutes the old man wondered if Claude were still there. He peeked shyly over the edge of the blanket, then quickly covered his face. Claude sat quietly.

A few more minutes, and another peek. Curiosity was getting the better of Jules Darnel. Tremulously, he asked, "What were you singing when you came up the stairs?"

"The song? Oh, that is a song to our Lady," and Claude began to sing again softly, "Laetare, O Maria!"

Bright tears came to the old man's eyes, and when Claude had finished he whispered, "I used to sing it when I was a boy — Claude, did you say?" Claude nodded his head, smiling.

"Claude, do you think you could come again tomorrow and sing to me? I . . . get very lonely."

"Yes, I'll come tomorrow and bring a friend."

The old man thought for a while.

"Yes, it is time I saw a priest. Yes, Claude, that is good."

The old man was no happier than Claude was to be able to bring a priest to this lonely old soul with the help he needed for his last days.

At a time like this Claude realized the meaning of his vocation and it seemed to grow dearer to him each day. But it puzzled him when he realized, also, that he undeniably felt more and more in his element in the fashionable gatherings where he could enjoy and take part in stimulating discussions. Among the guests at these glittering gatherings in the Colberts' circle there were people who would always remain Claude's friends. M. Patru was one of these. A member of the famed French Academy, he admired Claude's style of speech and writing and at one time remarked to a group that Claude was "one of those Frenchmen who has, to a superior degree, an understanding of the uses and beauties of the French language." This was high praise, coming from a professional educator.

Claude was flattered. It was true that he enjoyed the good opinion of others. Yet it was the good opinion of God which he had intended to gain. He knew only too well that human respect was the trap into which he could easily fall if he allowed himself to be vain enough.

His sincerity was revealed by the words he wrote in his journal: "You alone, my Savior, are worthy of being loved, served and praised. Fear of human respect is responsible even for doing good in order to please others. I shall do my duty and try to do good only because I desire to please You!" He set himself to paying more frequent visits to the poor and the sick, an antidote to vanity which he found very effective.

Claude talked one day to his two students about the Jesuit missions in New France. How far away these heroic missionaries seemed now! How easily at times he had accepted the luxuries of Paris, only to forget the scene of the Heart of Christ which he had so lately preached, the device of St. Francis de Sales who had strolled these very streets and halls.

Indeed, he had found little annoyance in this life. The sacrifices, if any existed, were paltry. He admitted to himself that he liked the atmosphere of culture, the position as tutor, the pleasant recreation and the social life among cultivated people.

His future as a Jesuit seemed to be assured, his greatest problem being to persevere in the avoidance of human respect.

The boys' lessons had been completed one afternoon at Sceaux, the new country estate, and a tennis game was in progress. All books had been left in the room which was reserved for Claude on his visits. Among them was a notebook lying open on the top of the table. Monsieur Colbert happened to stop at the doorway as he passed.

Glancing at the open notebook, he picked it up and read some lines which seemed to be in Claude's handwriting. It was an epigram:

Colbert has gotten out of the mud
And fears to fall back with a thud.

Anger tightened the chest and pounded in the head of this proud, self-sufficient man. He stamped down the long stairway and out onto the lawn where he confronted Claude.

Claude needed all his composure and dignity to withstand this attack. Where the couplet had originated, Claude was not certain. But there it was, and he was dismissed. No chance was given to defend himself — he who was so unfailingly courteous.

To Pere de Champs, who was deeply grieved, he said in anguish, "Father, am I unaware of what propriety demands of me when I have to deal with men?"

He felt that he had been strongly attached to life in Paris. But when word came of his transfer to Lyons, he was relieved and deeply pleased. He was to teach at La Trinite.

Later, he wrote in his notes, "You will have to suffer for years without anybody taking any notice of you. But if they should happen to see a fault they grumble, get angry and dismiss you."

And writing in his journal of just such an incident, he philosophized: "Without this accident you would never have been altogether bad, but perhaps you would never have been altogether good. You were unable to choose what would please God and what would please society and to make the necessary sacrifices."

So, Claude found even at this early period in his life that the world of wealth and glamor might not always deal well with one.

6.

Resolution

CLAUDE looked back to consider his life in religion up until this time. Had he improved? Had he swerved from his aims and intentions? Certainly, when he had been in the seminary in Avignon, he had been sheltered and had firm guidance. In Paris, there had been much exposure to worldly excitement. He had always been able to justify his pleasure in the glitter of wealth in the Colbert family as just a passing interlude into which he had been led by his peculiar assignment.

But how important to him had this way of life been? He was not sure. To be good one day and to give way to faults of vanity another day was not what Claude had intended. Perhaps the fiasco of the notebook, the accusations of Colbert, were good, after all. Perhaps he should be grateful that this mirror had been held up for him to see how much he must still do to perfect himself.

Lyons was an appropriate refuge to Claude at this time. Though a city of learning and cultivation, Lyons was not poisoned by the intrigue and undercurrents which so easily trapped the unwary. Besides, Lyons was familiar to him, and here there were people dear to him.

Humbert had married. His happy family and his wife's relatives welcomed Claude warmly. Frequent visits within this devoted family helped to heal the wounds of his unhappy experience with the Colberts.

- 55 -

Claude's younger brother, Joseph, had completed his law studies brilliantly. He would one day serve in the Jesuit Missions in New France, which had been one of Claude's early dreams.

Study took more and more of Claude's time each day, yet there was time to reacquaint himself with the old city. He strolled up and down the familiar streets, stopping once in a while to admire the view down upon the Rhone where it came rushing from the mountains to merge with the Saone. Riverboats and barges tied up at the river-level docks, some of them the very boats he had once watched at Vienne and at Avignon.

The streams and canals of France were busy in those days. Overland roads were apt to be muddy during three seasons, and dusty and rough in the summer. Many canals had been built to connect the main waterways, and King Louis and Colbert had others in mind for the future. Save for the tough and turbulent Rhone passage, water travel was more comfortable, cleaner, and not much slower than that by coach or by wagon.

Claude enjoyed the busy activities of the old city. He walked down the hill to the wharves one clear, cool day in late October, soon after his arrival in Lyons, to watch the stevedores as they worked. Shouts and cries filled the air already alive with the flapping of ropes and the raising and lowering of many-colored sails, the splashing and gurgling of water around and about the boats and piers, and the squeaking and groaning of vessels floating at anchor.

Casks of the wines of Burgundy and Provence were rolled out onto the docks to the lusty songs of the workers. Sacks of grain from Lorraine or Picardy were piled on wagons. What looked like confusion was really purposeful and productive employment.

One young man, dressed as a clerk and making notes in a book, seemed to watch Claude. Who was he? Claude walked closer to the wooden chests which were being so diligently counted and saw the address of "Andre La Belle, Silk Merchant," on each one. Of course! He turned to the youth, now recognized as the young cousin of his sister-in-law, Humbert's wife. Paul Charmot kept the accounting of

the shipments of silk for Andre La Belle, once a good friend of
Claude de la Colombiere.

Claude introduced himself. They talked about the ships and the
work involved. Together, the two ascended the street from the docks
toward Andre's shop.

"I have an idea, Paul. You go into the shop as though you did
not know me. We'll pay Andre a prank in his own coin."

And so, laughing, they parted in the street.

Claude walked unobtrusively through the door and looked
around. Counters near the windows held a few bolts of silk on
display, while the shelves held many others carefully wrapped in old
linen covers to protect the material from dust and from fading in the
light. Andre stood, looking sturdy and prosperous, showing blue, red
and dove-gray materials to a young woman.

"Oh, Monsieur La Belle, I am attracted to the gray. It's an
unusual shade and the soft shine is lovely."

"But, Madame Carre, the blue is beautiful, also. It almost
seems to be your color."

"Monsieur, one would not expect to be given such flattering
assistance in buying a piece of dress goods!"

"My business deals with color, Mme. Carre, and this blue is
like your eyes, if you have noticed. It would look striking on you in
the ballroom."

"You have convinced me. Send the material to my home
today."

Claude walked around, meanwhile, to the farther side of the
shop, eavesdropping gleefully. Ha! How gallant old Andre was!

No sooner had the young matron left the shop than Claude
turned and approached the proprietor now engrossed in rolling and
covering the precious silk.

Claude spoke, "How little did we suspect the talents we would
develop through the years. I wouldn't have missed this little scene for
the world, Andre. What a gallante you have turned out to be!"

Andre, startled, rushed toward Claude and threw his arms

about him. They shouted as though they were young boys at school again.

"Claude, Claude! How good to see you. Humbert said you were back in Lyons but were busy. How did you come here?"

"I ran into Paul down by the docks. Where is the boy?"

"Here in the office, enjoying the spectacle we're giving him. But seriously, my wife, Nancy, has ordered the gray, and these two young matrons are rivals. I wouldn't dare sell the gray to Mme. Carre. Besides, Nancy, with her black hair and her peach and cream complexion, will be exquisite in it."

"What complicated problems you married men must have. Now, do you see how lucky I am, Andre, in my state of life? But tell me; what is the event so important that your security hinges on the color your wife may wear?"

"Claude, come home to lunch with me, and we'll tell you all about it."

Leaving the shop in good hands, Andre led Claude out into the street and toward his home.

Lunch was pleasant, served by Nancy, who led the conversation.

"All the women in Lyons are preparing a reception at the College for the Italian princess, Mary Beatrice d'Este," she said.

"Yes, Claude, you never heard of so much secrecy and intrigue." He glanced teasingly at his wife. "Did you ever hear of a wine shampoo? Well — you are now 'in' on one of the great beauty secrets. It's supposed to bring out the glow in a woman's hair. And the dresses! If you hire a seamstress who also works for other families, be cautious what you let her know. She may be offered bribes to tell the others what you are going to wear."

Claude laughed. "After Paris, I should not be surprised, but I didn't really expect this in Lyons!"

"Lyons!" Andre pretended to bridle. "Lyons, I will have you know, is almost as proud of social leadership as Paris!"

"Isn't Mary Beatrice the daughter of the awesome Mary of

Modena? Father had a client whose ears were clipped back properly on a wine and wheat exchange with her."

"Yes, but this princess is quite different. She had not planned to marry but to enter a Visitation convent. We shall have a time keeping her away from the Bellecour Convent long enough to appear at the reception in her honor!

"You saw some of my chests of silk on the dock this morning, Claude. Some of that is on its way to Bernard LaBelle, my cousin, in Modena.

"Bernard attended the proxy wedding when Mary Beatrice married the Duke of York, Prince James of England. It was *the* big event of the year in this part of Europe. I just wish I had been able to see some of the silks worn there! Bernard said that much of it came from India."

"Now you're talking shop! How did the princess decide to marry English royalty?"

"It was King Louis' doing, really. He thought it would cement friendship between England, France and the Roman States to unite these two young people. Mary Beatrice wasn't convinced until Pope Clement advised her to consent."

"Poor child!" murmured Nancy. "To think of marrying an unknown, absent groom and traveling to a far, unfriendly country. But at least 'The Cromwell' is no longer alive."

"Yes, Nancy. Andre has told me of your early morning walks to Mass across the park from here. Suppose that military police stood at all such corners to report you for your attendance. These remnants of Cromwell's work still exist in England and, seriously, one can lose all one's property or be exiled or imprisoned if the mood of the crowd turns against one."

Again Nancy sighed, "Poor child!" Then turning to her husband she said, "Why don't you show Claude your maps of New France? I will have to see that the children are settled for their naps."

And Claude followed Andre to his study, thinking what a delightful family this was, and how good it was to see Andre again.

It was not until the evening of the big reception for Mary Beatrice that Claude, chaperoning a group of younger students, saw how fully Andre rejoiced in his life. "No taint of Jansenism can be found in old Andre, certainly," he thought with an affectionate chuckle.

The Duchess Mary Beatrice had, indeed, visited the Visitation Convent of Bellecour, as Nancy had predicted she would. But no desire for escape had prompted her in her devotion. In her visits at Bellecour she viewed the relics of St. Francis de Sales, whose heart was preserved there. She repeatedly expressed, when talking to Claude or one of the nuns, or to a dear or trusted friend, that her refuge was "in the side of Jesus." Her loneliness in thinking of her new home in far-off England caused her to speak of this devotion which St. Francis de Sales had held dear, thus establishing a bond between herself and Claude, who, also, often thought in terms of the writings of St. Francis.

She was interested in the vocation of Claude's younger sister, Marguerite, in the Visitation Order. She was concerned that there would not be priests in England. "And what, then, shall I do, with no means to nurture the faith of my husband and family?"

Such modesty and devotion to duty gave Claude a key to her character. In years to come this was to be of great assistance to both of them.

In a few days she departed from Lyons, having made a deep impression upon many of the acquaintances she had made in her short stay. Aboard the fitted barge that was as pretty as a little cottage and later, while being carried over the mountains in her sedan chair, she wrote to friends of her desire to use her life in helping others.

The time was now approaching when Claude would be ordained. The third year, or tertianship, when he would be assisted in carrying out a "prolonged meeting of the whole man with Jesus" had arrived. In the secluded quiet of St. Joseph's, the seminary year of 1674-1675 began.

Thirty days of uninterrupted silence brought a new experience to Claude. He put aside the books he had chosen as his own favorites and turned to those selected by his spiritual father. *The Spiritual Exercises of St. Ignatius* provided the basis for his long retreat.

His meditations led him into exploring one phase of his personality which had caused him deep concern. He remembered how often he had delighted in the friendships he had made: in the classrooms in Lyons and Avignon; in social gatherings; in the entourage of a French Prime Minister who had esteemed him; in his circle of teaching friends.

He thought of the pleasure he had taken in music and the arts. Most of all, his own ability and achievement had been cause for pride and vainglory. He realized that he possessed a deep, abiding love of praise.

Would it not be better for him to withdraw altogether from the conflict and combat of worldly life? How much more sincere could one be than to retreat from any occasion of sin? One course lay open to him. One of the approved means in such a problem was to apply for a transfer to the Carthusian Order. How sweetly this would settle his dilemma! To pray in a quiet, secluded chapel! To walk in a quiet, cloistered garden! To meditate, read, and study! A heaven on earth — no spiritual pitfalls, no danger of vainglory.

With an effort which cost him days of anguish, he withdrew from this way of thinking. The example of St. Francis de Sales, of Isaac Jogues, of Pierre Lallemont must prevail for him, he knew. His Order was involved in missionary work, in work for the salvation of neighbors, and in preaching and teaching. In one of these fields, he would find his fulfillment.

What were the many temptations he would be exposing himself to? To seek self was dangerous; therefore, he must deny himself and his desires sternly. What had been the reply of St. Bernard in just such a crisis? Said St. Bernard to the demon tempting him, "It was not for you that I began, and it will not be for you that I will stop!"

And yet, as simply as it could be stated, this conflict could not be fought out so easily. He came to feel that the most terrible trials would be easier than this living death of complete detachment. How endless this struggle could be. Could he *ever* accomplish perfection?

As the days went on and he found he had improved himself in the practice of the presence of God, he began to be consoled. He resolved to persevere in this exercise so that he might act to please God rather than those around him. And so, bursting from his heart came a plea, "Dear God, I wish to make myself holy — just between you and me!"

The struggle was not ended at this time, nor so easily, for it would continue for a long, long time to come. Would he withstand the demands of his own nature? Would he succeed in his own immolation? While there is life, the struggle goes on. If he might resolve to love from day to day, he might win the contest. He dared, as he wrote, "to hope that one will die in harness, at whatever cost, to please God."

And then a premonition came to him. How could he bear it if he were imprisoned, loaded with chains, discredited? After some terror, he placed this possibility also in the hands of God and made this entreaty, "If ever my heart should please You, take it then!" He likened himself to a piece of charcoal which a painter uses to sketch upon his canvas before painting a picture, then throws into the fire when he has no further need for it. Surely, he thought, God would not use him to help save souls and then discard him to the flames of hell; God was too good. But in spite of all these fears and apprehensions about the faults he saw in himself, it was to prove in later years that he never broke the heroic vow he took at this time to reject the world and to satisfy God at any cost. It was a fact that his superiors had no doubts concerning him, and that they had confidence in his abilities and his blameless religious life.

At the time of his ordination, his brothers in religion regarded him as one destined for a pulpit in a large city parish. And so, it developed that the most surprising appointment of the year was that of Father Claude de la Colombiere to the little Jesuit College at

Paray-le-Monial. If Claude had been looking for a humble station, surely this was it, as he wrote to Andre upon leaving Lyons:

"My dear friend, if one needed to hide one's self and withdraw from the affairs of men, I cannot think of a better place to go. What excitement could ever come from a convent?

"It is with regret that I do leave Lyons. The visits with you and your family have been important to me. And, Andre, never change. You are a credit to your family and your friends. How little trouble Jansenism would give if all were as happy and as enthusiastic as you!"

7.

Margaret Mary

IT was a wiser, more recollected Claude than the youth who had traveled to Paris who, at the age of thirty-four, now followed the road from Lyons to Paray-le-Monial, where he would be chaplain at the Priory and Municipal College and, in addition, spiritual director to the nuns in the Convent of the Visitation. His half-joking lines to Andre, "What excitement could come from a convent?" revealed to him now that he had felt, perhaps, just a touch of pique, and that he was still vulnerable, though he meant most sincerely and deeply to adhere to his vow. The meaning of his vocation became increasingly clear to him. The challenge of intellectual repartee, the thrill that he might feel in seeing the gold and glitter of wealth — these were not for him. They never had been. But in Paris, he had allowed himself to be taken in by the charm of it all.

After his long retreat, he could see more clearly. He must try to correspond with grace, and now that he had again found God as his supreme goal, he must act as though he did, and think in the same terms. Else, how could he be true to himself? Thus, it was with a true sense of gratitude and of the fitness of this assignment in the eyes of God that he proceeded to Paray.

In this bleak little monastic city he was to find the Providence of God awaiting him in a very real way, and it was destined to prove more challenging than anything he could have dreamed of earlier.

For in the convent where he was to be spiritual director, there lived a young sister named Margaret Mary Alacoque whom God had chosen as one of his special friends.

On this February day in 1675 while Claude was making his way across the little city, Sister Margaret Mary was walking within the cloistered walls. From the slope of the land she could only see beyond the convent buildings to the tower of St. Nicholas in the distance. She knew that nearby would be the low buildings of the Benedictine Priory that priory whose church had been built as a model for the construction of the famous Abbey Church of Cluny nine hundred years before. Above the main altar there was a marvelous medieval fresco of Christ the King — a famed relic of long ago fortunately spared by Huguenot raiders of the last century.

Cold as the garden was, the quiet and solitude were a relief from the hubbub inside during this recreation period.

"To come out walking alone in the garden reminds me of my girlhood days," Margaret Mary thought, smiling.

But it was with a small pang that she realized it was not a joke at all. She was not meant to be a person who made friends easily. This alone made her the target of those who resented her "difference."

Margaret Mary Alacoque was the daughter of a lawyer of Verosvres in Burgundy who had died young and in debt, and an ailing mother who had been too meek to resist the encroachments and abuses of aggressive relatives who had moved in after her husband's death. Margaret Mary's acute need to escape these kinfolk for a few minutes now and then had led to much trouble. The loud, abusive language and sneers of the aunt and cousins had often made her cringe.

There had been a rock on the hillside, an ancient rock carved out by wind and rain, in which she could hide and, kneeling, look down into the valley directly upon the little country church. From afar, but within sight, she could fulfill her need to adore the Blessed Sacrament which she knew to be behind those walls.

No one had ever been able to find her there. She took good care never to lead them to this little cave nor to reveal where she had been. But how many times her courage was saved in this hidden shelter, only she knew.

Even here in the convent she was unable to resist this ever-growing impulse to drop a broom, a duster or a scrubbing brush, to rush to the chapel. Her Lord needed to be adored. She needed to adore him. It was as simple as that.

So, why did other nuns find her life's work strange? Were they not nuns? Were they not also cloistered? Why did they find it so unusual that she must spend extra minutes and extra hours in prayer? It was for this she had come to this shelter, this convent.

The measured steps of the petite nun did not betray her feelings as she thought of the problems which she had certainly not expected to meet at the convent of Paray-le-Monial.

The sisters said she was presumptuous in passing on the messages which her Lord asked her to give to the sisters. No one could have been less willing than she to do it. She had protested. She had tried to misunderstand. She had procrastinated. But there had been no escape from his importunate will.

Yes, she had, upon command of her Lord, reproached them for their lukewarm faith, for their lack of charity. In this she had seemed no better than they who criticized her.

Surely, under the circumstances, Margaret Mary could not take offense if they nudged each other and whispered about her prayers, or even if they sprinkled holy water on her to "drive out the devil from her."

The hardest of all was when Abbe Michon from the church of St. Nicholas told her to eat more food and she "would not imagine these visions."

But recently her Lord had said to her, "I will soon send you my faithful servant and perfect friend in whom you may confide." Would the new chaplain expected within a few days be the one she might talk with? He sounded so young, so — almost frivolous!

"I must not think about this," she reproved herself, turning toward the recreation room entrance. The angelus bell sounded and the movement toward the chapel distracted attention from her.

Word went around the next day that Father Claude de la Colombiere had arrived at the Jesuit residence and would make his first visit to the Visitation Convent at Vespers that day.

Margaret Mary had been given a shawl to darn. She sat beside a window where the light was best.

Sister Francesca held herself to be the model of social courtesies. When she stopped beside Margaret Mary, she spoke more with the air of condescension than charity.

"Oh, Sister!" she exclaimed. "You darn so smoothly and so neatly. I'm sure our shawl will be even more useful when you finish."

"Thank you, Sister," Margaret Mary answered evenly, "it will be useful for a little while longer."

Beaming with admiration for herself for her great friendliness, Sister Francesca was soon sitting beside Sister Katherine, a ponderous, dissatisfied lady who suspected Margaret Mary to be possessed by the devil.

Sister Francesea opened the subject of Father Claude, one eye on Margaret Mary.

"My uncle is a farmer out in the Bois de Boulogne. Every Tuesday he sent three wagons of firewood to the Colbert home in Paris. He often heard the cook's son talk about the tutor of the Colbert sons, Father de la Colombiere, who was not yet ordained. Henri, the boy, often practiced reading with Father de la Colombiere while the Colbert boys studied. Cook said that Father de la Colombiere enjoyed fine parties to which he was often invited, and had many rides in the handsome Colbert coach. He likes to talk with lively and witty people. And he even drinks a cup of chocolate sometimes."

"I have heard," sniffed Sister Katherine, "that the Jesuit Order had banned the drinking of chocolate."

Sister Margaret Mary let this exchange pass over her head, as it were, for it was much like the talk of the past few days, only too well known. But at supper Sister Francesca inquired, "Sister Margaret Mary, do you think Father de la Colombiere will make us a successful chaplain?"

All eyes turned toward her, and many were puzzled by her answer which came in a quiet broken only by the rubbing of wooden spoons upon crockery bowls as the nuns ate their evening porridge. It was, "I am sure he will help us if we try to be helped."

When the bell sounded for Vespers, the whispering began.

The little nun walked meekly with her head down and eyes averted from the excited ones, desiring not to be disturbed, especially now. But murmurs came to her ears.

She clasped her hands just a little tighter. How could she avoid offending?

A tall, graceful figure presently appeared in the candlelit sanctuary. Murmurs and rustlings of curiosity were the only sounds in the chapel. Sister Margaret Mary Alacoque glanced up from her devotions and heard quite distinctly within her own heart, "This is he whom I have sent you."

If Margaret Mary had been sophisticated enough to have known about St. Teresa of Avila, she might have quoted the exasperated words of that great saint, "No wonder you have so few friends, Lord, if this is how you treat them." But she certainly felt frustrated, for how could a priest so young help her with her complicated problem? Should she again risk unbelief and rebuffs by revealing the words of her Blessed Lord? And yet, Jesus, her Lord, never deceived her. There was always a purpose in his words and so she must believe.

As for Claude, he noticed the one face in the community which wore, not the simple stare of curiosity, but the intense preoccupation of thoughtful study.

This look was the first recollection he had when he awoke the next morning. He thought, "My instructions included an unusual circumstance existing at Paray. I wonder what Mother Saumaise can tell me about it? Does it have to do with this unusual countenance?"

Claude learned from Mother Saumaise that Sister Margaret

Mary Alacoque, the visionary, who was the "unusual problem" was, indeed, the girl of the earnest face.

"What discipline have you applied to this sister, Mother Saumaise? Surely if she is kept busy, she will have little time to think so deeply."

"She has been given enough back-breaking tasks to discourage a strong woman. It makes no impression upon her, Father."

"How does she describe her visions?"

"She talks about the Heart of Christ, the Heart of Jesus. He talks to her, she claims."

"Mother Saumaise, where did Sister Margaret Mary hear about the Sacred Heart? What books does she read?"

"Father, she does not read. She is too busy working and praying to have time to read. And poor Abbe Michon only said, 'Nonsense!' What can I do?"

"This is an unusual story. A private and personal devotion to the Heart of Jesus does exist but it is almost unknown. Only a few people have been attracted to it. I cannot believe that Sister has even heard of it."

Father Claude walked to the window and looked over the dormant garden, thinking. After a while he queried, "Is Sister Alacoque apt to be emotional? You have convinced me she is not afraid of hard work, nor does she try to evade it."

"There is only one thing that causes her to weep and become ill, Father. I didn't believe or understand it myself for a long time, but I do now. She becomes very ill if she has to eat cheese."

"Cheese? She doesn't like it?"

"It isn't a case of liking. It causes her to be nauseated and faint. Her entire family is affected this way. I found this out when her brother Chrysostom visited her last year. But I am ashamed to say that she was, for a while, forced to try to eat it, because I ignored her pleas and allowed the refectory mistress to order her to eat it. She tried as many times as they demanded her obedience. But each time she ate cheese she was really ill."

As though he had forgotten the subject of their conversation, Claude remarked, "That's a sturdy donkey in the barnyard."

Mother Saumaise startled him by laughing heartily as if it gave her relief from her problems to do so. Claude turned and smiled, expecting an amusing story about the donkey. He was not entirely disappointed.

"That is the donkey we gave into Sister Alacoque's care last summer as one of her tasks. I sent her out to watch the donkey and its foal, to let the animals graze but not harm the vegetable garden.

"The chapel wall is nearby. Sister went over and knelt down close to it to pray, knowing herself to be close to the Blessed Sacrament. From a window I saw the animals having a feast in the beets and carrots while she was absorbed in her adoration."

Mother Saumaise gripped the edge of the table in her earnestness. "Father, I am not a dreamer. Sister Gertrude saw it, too. The animals bulged with good food.

"But when I walked out to take her to task, I had to interrupt her deepest prayer. Then it was my turn to be surprised. She looked around and said, 'Mother, they have done no damage.'

"Father, when I looked again, every row was growing thickly and the ground was smooth. She cannot be punished. She knows only prayer."

And so Claude was appointed confessor to Margaret Mary. Gradually, through many discussions leading to mutual understanding, the little nun felt more confident that she would find help through this priest.

It was necessary for him to decide how to deal wisely with her visions or to decide whether they were illusions.

Claude asked her, "Sister Margaret Mary, how did these occurrences begin? Was it after you entered this convent?"

"No, Father Colombiere. It began when I was very young. I promised the Blessed Mother when I was a small girl that I would give my life to her Son. I have always talked with them."

Claude felt an eerie feeling creep over him. If this girl spoke truthfully, this was a more complicated enigma than he had known. Was it, as one priest had reported, caused by a nervous disorder? If so, she would probably resent pain and discomfort. He could ask about this.

"Mother Saumaise told me that you are ill with fevers and pain quite often. Does this worry you?"

"Yes, Father, it bothers me to be the cause of so much disturbance. If they would not worry over me so much and let me hide away until I am well! I am so ashamed of causing this hardship among the sisters."

"But the pain itself; doesn't it make you unhappy?"

"Oh, no, Father! If you could only see how terribly our Lord suffered, you would know that he needs us to help him to bear the pain he suffers for us!"

"Has he given you some particular pain?"

"Father, Jesus touched my side and made an opening. He took my heart out of my side and reached it into his own side. I saw it burning within the vast space of his flaming Heart. He brought out my burning heart and placed it back into my side. It burns and pains. He promised it will never stop."

"Have you told this to the other sisters?"

"Only to Mother Saumaise. I don't think she believes me. But my Lord told me to tell her.

"I want to tell you about the notes, too, Father."

"The notes?"

"Yes. He told me to write to certain sisters and give them the notes telling them to give more attention to their prayers, or to observe the rule more carefully, or to give stricter attention to the silence. They have become very angry with me. But if I don't do it, my Lord is even more angry."

Pere Claude smiled when he thought of these sisters so proud and righteous being told how to behave by Sister Margaret Mary. "Try giving the notes to Mother Saumaise instead. She will decide what to do with them, Sister."

Claude decided that a journal written by Margaret Mary should record her entire mystical life and all her thoughts and actions. A study of this journal might lead to a solution of how her superior should deal with her and to help Claude to advise her more sensibly.

Margaret Mary objected. It would not only be difficult for her but it would take precious hours from her life of contemplation. Claude told her it was necessary, that without an exact account he could not possibly judge what had happened. At last, reluctantly, she agreed. She didn't see why so much fuss was being made over her troubles. She didn't feel that she was important. It was only that she must pass on the messages given to her, she protested.

In all of this, Claude found no indication of a desire to deceive. Margaret Mary, uneducated, meek and humble, surely possessed simplicity. As for her problems, he recalled what St. John Berchmans had said, "Community life is the greatest of mortifications." Perhaps the discipline of writing would help the nun to see things in a different light; perhaps she could take her experiences less seriously.

8.

The Flaming Heart

"HOW gradually and imperceptibly a life can change," Claude thought as he walked through the meadow path near the River Bourbince from the Jesuit College to the Convent of the Visitation. In the few months since he first arrived in Paray this meadow had changed from a dry, frozen place to a verdant, flowery Easter garden.

What was it he had written to Andre upon leaving Lyons? "What excitement could one hope to find in a convent?"

Excitement, let it be admitted, was not the same for all people. He remembered the time when the thrill of writing a perfect sermon had exceeded all else. To this, Claude had added the conquest of himself. He felt that even these objectives were to be changed, perhaps little, perhaps much. Sermons must be enriched, expounded, from the experience of the writer and his deepening thoughts.

He had in mind the letter received from his young sister, Marguerite, who, in the Visitation Convent at Condrieu, had been having great difficulty in adjusting to community life and in feelings of anguish at leaving her aging and ailing father, Bertrand. A small frown came to Claude's brows when he recalled that Marguerite had spent some of her most impressionable years deprived of her mother. This could make a difference. He must write to her with loving brotherly advice, and very soon.

And then, underlining this progress which human events have a way of making was the one which really concerned him most — Sister Margaret Mary Alacoque's visions. Having been absent from Paray for a few weeks to conduct the Lenten Mission at the Abbey la Benissons-Dieu, he could return to this puzzling condition with a fresh mind. He hoped Sister Alacoque had found a new self-discipline and gained more control over her emotions. Writing her journal each day should help her greatly. If his sympathy for her and his advice had settled her problem, he would be well satisfied. How wisely had it been said that no devotion in the Church could ever be based upon private revelation alone.

Margaret Mary Alacoque might surely have her own love for the Sacred Heart of Jesus as long as it did not disturb the life of the community about her. In this she would be emulating St. Francis de Sales, St. Gertrude, St. John Eudes and countless others.

When he arrived at the convent, Mother Saumaise was expecting him. Her face was drawn. It seemed that wrinkles had seated themselves on her brow in those weeks, while her mouth had a sterner look and her eyes mirrored a deep concern.

"Mother Saumaise! Have you been ill?"

"Not really, Father. But I have had some difficulty. Would you come into my office, please?"

"Mother, this must be serious. Does it concern you or Sister Alacoque?"

"Father, I must first admit to you that I have doubted Sister Margaret Mary in the past. I have scolded her and often caused her great humiliation. But to my amazement she has proved to be humble and obedient by nature. She is persistent in what she believes. She is *not* self-seeking nor weak.

"Her problems have led this convent into turmoil, but at last I can give her my complete sympathy and confidence." Mother Saumaise scowled at a bumble bee buzzing on the outside of a window pane.

"There has been a terrible outbreak of gossip and back-biting

against Sister since you left. I have heard rumors and I have over-
heard some of the talk as I worked. I have seen the tear-stained face
of Sister. Her bearing has grown gradually more humble, more meek
and, at times, quite defeated.

"But Sister Margaret Mary can take this. She simply prays and
contemplates, and today's troubles fade away, leaving her ready to
face whatever may come tomorrow."

Mother Saumaise folded her hands tightly and looked at Claude
with a worried expression. He waited.

"I know I am having a terrible time in coming to the object of my
effort, but I'm sure you'll see why. Please don't be shocked."

"Why no, Mother. It is quite hard to shock me, really. Try me
and see." And he chuckled, though a little nervously.

"The story, briefly, Father, is that some of the nuns are sure
that you yourself, Father de la Colombiere, miss the excitement and
the social life of Paris; that you have had such excellent assignments
in Paris and Lyons that Paray is obviously an assignment of boredom
to you. Now, don't look so angry! I must finish this, so that we can
find some solution to this trouble.

"They say that the possibility of guiding a mystic is intriguing to
you, and that you are easy prey because of this quixotic state of
affairs. They can see, so the story goes, just how easy it is for Sister to
take advantage of you and get you to listen to her!

"There! I didn't think I could face you with this. I didn't think
you would hear me out."

And, surprising herself, Mother Saumaise found tears rolling
down her cheeks. She reached for her handkerchief and patted them
away. Then she looked at Claude.

He sat as still as a statue. She was not sure whether it was anger
or horror that shone from his eyes. He placed his hands on the arms of
his chair and pushed himself up as though he were an old man.
Staring, he walked to the window.

"Father!" she exclaimed. "I am sorry. So sorry."

"Don't, Mother Saumaise. I tell you, Sister Margaret Mary is a chosen soul. In some way, though, we may be deceiving ourselves. I must think.

"It was your duty to tell me this. We could be bringing reproach upon your Order and upon mine. We could be responsible for causing scandal by our way of proceeding.

"Consider, Mother Saumaise, that the tongue has been placed in a cage, surrounded by strong teeth and firmly shut in by a pair of lips. And yet, it is the cause of more trouble than you or I could foresee. Gossip, slander, idle talk — not one is good. We can't take the chance of misleading weak people.

"Let me come back tomorrow. I will talk with you and with Sister. I may be able to give you an answer."

Claude turned, left the office. He walked as one weighed down by a heavy burden. Was he being deceived by Margaret Mary? He could not believe her to be clever and devious as the sisters indicated. Even Mother Saumaise, the clear-eyed and levelheaded one, believed.

Voices came to him from the other side of the tall hedge where the sisters' recreation was taking place.

"Sister, do you have the holy water?"

"Yes, right here in my pocket. Here's a little flask."

"Now, when we sprinkle it on her as we walk around that way, don't forget the words of the exorcism to drive out the devil, 'Be gone, Deceiver,' and be sure the water goes on her."

The two voices faded, leaving Claude on his side of the hedge to fight a wretched cold chill. Immediately the brisk voice of Sister Francesca came to him, "Sister, did you know that Father de la Colombiere is with Mother Saumaise *at this moment*? I wonder if he is being undeceived at last?

"What a pity for such a fine young priest to be so misled!" Her voice implied sympathy for anyone, it would seem, excepting Sister Margaret Mary Alacoque.

Another voice murmured, "Sister Alacoque picked up my scissors when I dropped them yesterday and handed them to me. I thanked her, but I find it most difficult to be friendly. I must say I don't like the 'messages' about charity she gives us!"

Sister Francesca snickered nervously, "Poor Sister, don't take it so seriously!" and the two voices faded out of range.

Claude had loitered deliberately during this exchange and had heard enough to convince him of the need to study Sister Alacoque's claims as intensely as possible.

Still seething with indignation and struck by the lack of charity he had witnessed, perhaps a little guilty for fear of his own share in not seeing all this, Claude sat down at his desk in the Jesuit College and penned a letter to his little sister Marguerite. His brotherly advice grew quite serious. He wrote, "The good of the world depends on the thoroughness with which each one fulfills the duties of his state in life. Many religious keep the rule because the bell rings, and others go to this duty or that. Communities which should be furnaces where one is continually set on fire with the love of God remain in shocking tepidity. Do not, my sister, try to change others. Do *your* duty well, and you may find that you serve as an example to others."

The next morning he told Mother Saumaise, "We will continue as we are. I doubt that any words of ours will change the cruel tongues or thoughtless minds very quickly. . . . Please tell Sister Alacoque to continue with her journal, and I will ask her for it in a few days."

At Mass, Claude turned to pronounce the "Lord, I am not worthy." Sister Margaret Mary Alacoque's pale, upturned face was transfixed as "of one beholding a great vision." She seemed unaware of all around her for many minutes, remaining as if dazed. It was difficult to persuade her to leave the chapel.

Claude hoped that she would tell him what had happened. He himself was distracted. How could he find a way to understand her better?

One day after Claude had read his office for the day, he went to the chapel, hoping for guidance in his problem.

Reverently he knelt before the Blessed Sacrament.

He let his mind go back over all that he knew, all that he had heard, all he had ever thought about the Heart of Christ. It seemed to him that a great swell of music made a background for his thoughts. Loving music as he did, a great musical pageant arose in his mind.

Above the majestic harmony of liturgical praise to God the Father, God the Son, and God the Holy Spirit, there arose, sometimes strongly, sometimes almost unheard, an insistent melody of love for the Heart of Jesus. On Calvary, as the spear of the Roman soldier pierced this Heart — where only the day before the head of John, the beloved disciple, had bowed and rested with love and familiarity — blood and water flowed out, an unforgettable symbol of healing and salvation to all.

Early in the first centuries of the Church that music of adoration for the pierced Heart of Christ arose from such religious leaders as St. Justin Martyr and St. Sanctus of Lyons. St. John Chrysostom took up the song, and it passed to St. Ambrose, renowned for his hymns.

The praise passed on to St. Augustine, and through many tongues and countries it reached St. Thomas. All of these and many more had kept that heavenly melody throbbing and beating. It could be recognized in their writings. It could be felt in their works. It was no new song, this love for the wounded Heart of Christ, but old as Redemption itself. Claude, in his meditation on the continuing influence of a fragile, unofficial, private devotion, was struck with wonder at the way it reached into the mind and soul of Sister Margaret Mary.

She was certainly no student, knew little of the Gospels, much less of Church history or of philosophy. Unless by some casual reference in a sermon or two during her lifetime, she could scarcely have heard of this devotion. What was the reason for her torment? Was she to be an instrument as St. Francis of Assisi had been? What did the Lord want of her? What, of him?

This would be the hour when Sister Margaret Mary would be in her cell, writing.

Writing so precisely was a difficult skill she had not cultivated, nor seemed to need. The subject of her mystical experiences was a hard one to relate.

The light was not very clear. Her newly sharpened quill squeaked on the paper. The ink which Sister Apothecary had shown her how to mix was faded looking. She wrote, "I am a burning candle before the Blessed Sacrament. My greatest wish is for my life to be consumed like a lighted candle before my Beloved."

"My Lord said to me, 'My divine Heart is so impassioned with love for humankind and for you in particular that, unable any longer to contain the flames of Its burning charity, they must be spread abroad to you. I have chosen you as an abyss of unworthiness and ignorance to carry out this great design, so that all may be done by me alone.' "

"It was then that my Lord placed my heart within his Heart. I shall wear this burning pain always."

"Later he told me that he demands reparation for coldness and rebuffs. He said, 'Receive me in the Blessed Sacrament as often as obedience allows. . . . You will also receive Holy Communion the first Friday of every month and every Thursday night I will make you share the deadly sadness I felt in the Garden of Olives. . . . You will rise between eleven and midnight to prostrate yourself for an hour with me, lying on your face, so to appease the divine anger by demanding mercy for sinners and to sweeten to some extent the bitterness I felt at my abandonment by my disciples.' "

"On the Feast of Corpus Christi I saw the Sacred Heart exposed. Again he spoke to me, 'Behold this Heart which has so loved men and women, has spared nothing, even to suffering and death, to show them its love.' "

" 'And instead of gratitude, I receive for the most part nothing but ingratitude, irreverence and sacrilege, coldness and contempt which they show to me in the sacrament of Love.' "

" 'I ask that the first Friday after the Octave of Corpus Christi be dedicated to a special feast in honor of my Heart, in reparation for the indignities it has suffered while exposed on altars.' "

When Claude read this — and all the entries she had made in these past weeks, his finely arched brows rose higher and higher; his eyes took on a look of wonder.

Marvelous to think of, Sister Margaret Mary Alacoque was possessed of a complete devotion and philosophy and an entire method of teaching the practice of a liturgical devotion to the Sacred Heart of Jesus to the whole world! It was stated in the most awesome accents and with unequivocal authority. The two great commands of Jesus could be unmistakably understood: love and reparation. Only one answer could be found: this girl was one chosen to see and hear what others in her generation did not dare to imagine.

True as were her visions, and simple as was her faith, she would never know how her every sentence harmonized with the devotion through the ages.

A feeling of awe caused him to bow his head as warm tears rushed to his eyes. Pity for this mystic nun held him astonished. The way of a mystic was never easy, he reflected, and prayed, "Oh, sacred, holy Heart of Jesus, may she have the grace of perseverance and the fortitude to endure all!"

The judicial mind he had inherited from his lawyer ancestors stood him in good stead in studying the complete report. He was now thoroughly convinced. He wrote a note to Sister Margaret Mary in care of Mother Saumaise. He told her that he believed in her mission. From that time on she could depend upon his help in her work for the divine Heart.

To Mother Saumaise, Claude offered some practical advice. He said, "This is no invention of Sister Margaret Mary. This is a gift of God. You should encourage the First Friday devotion and the Holy Hour."

To which Mother Saumaise questioned, "What can be done about the rest of the community? How should they regard this devotion?"

"I think they should observe these devotions only if they really want to, and after talking with you. As time goes on, others will be convinced."

Margaret Mary and Claude formally consecrated themselves to the Sacred Heart on the following Friday. Margaret Mary, inside the grille, and Claude at the altar, knew this to be a serious occasion.

When Margaret Mary came to Holy Communion she was shown the Heart of Jesus once again. This time it burned fiercely; and then in this Heart she was shown two other hearts, her own and Claude's. She heard these words, "Thus my pure love unites forever these three hearts!"

9.

Special Talent

"THERE is more virtue in that house than one might think," Claude stated firmly. He sturdily defended the Visitation Convent.

Eager ears had heard the talk of the bedevilment of Sister Margaret Mary. Greedy eyes had peeked at her from across the Bourbince River while she toiled at washing linens on the river bank and at loading the wet garments into panniers on the back of the donkey, to be taken to the garden for drying. Townspeople had even gone to the chapel and peered through the grille hoping to see the little sister in ecstasy.

It was no wonder that the people of Paray-le-Monial and nearby Romay and Charolles should think that weird and terrible things went on in "that convent."

Since the number of students in the college was small and the duties here and at the Visitation Convent were not numerous, even if one included the fact that Paray was a base from which Father Claude was assigned to missions and preaching duties in the surrounding parishes, some hours each week could be spent in what could be described as parish work about the town.

With a few words here, and a few there, Claude talked with people; he organized sodalities among the men and boys, and while he preached, he directed the thoughts of people away from criticism and intemperate gossip.

He preached one favorite theme in varied words and phrases. This idea seemed to be necessary to a spirit of charity. On one occasion he said it in this way: "Simplicity helps us to forget our own virtues, and humility persuades us that others have virtues also. Dear God, what a sad occupation, examining the lives of one's neighbors! A heart filled with the love of God has something much better to do!"

Gradually, through the months, Margaret Mary was spared ever more and more from the lashing tongues and the sly, cruel actions she had known.

The Visitation Convent now became known for pious lives instead of unkindness. Those many sisters who had never taken part in the rash deeds now had a calm atmosphere in which to practice the true devotion which was their vocation. Claude thought of them when he wrote, "Among these sisters I have found persons of so lofty a holiness that I have never known greater virtue."

Having in mind the urgent desire of the Sacred Heart for more frequent communions, Father Colombiere made it clear that he wanted people to show greater devotion to Mass and the Blessed Sacrament, in order to share in its blessings. And he never forgot the complaint of our Lord to Sister Margaret Mary: "What is most disheartening is the infidelity of hearts that are consecrated to me."

Claude threw his energy into sermons and writing, but the force of his presence was very effective and brought about changes in the lives of a number of individuals. One remarkable case of this kind took place in connection with the Ursuline school for girls in Paray. Anne-Alexis was the youngest daughter of Madame de Mareschelle, an abjured Calvinist converted to Catholicism. Anne-Alexis was taken to the Ursuline Convent by her mother who feared that the older daughters, still Calvinists, had set themselves the task of saving Anne-Alexis from "popery." They had, however, already strongly influenced the younger girl, and she had to be removed from the convent because of emotional outbursts against the nuns.

Later, Anne-Alexis thought she was merely making a visit to

the Visitation Convent. But when she discovered that her mother had quietly departed, leaving her to stay as a boarder, she went into a rage. Running and screaming, she shouted, "Cut off my head! I'd rather die than become a Papist and stay with these wolves and devils of religious!"

Mme. Mareschelle begged Claude to visit the child and to talk to her to calm her emotions.

Before he was able to do so, the girl was walking in the garden one day when she was attracted strangely to a tree in its springtime foliage. She pictured it, in her frantic state, as a way of escape. She climbed the tree with a rope in her hand.

She eased herself out on one of the branches and with the determination of desperation, tied one end of the rope to a branch and threw the other over the high wall.

Mother Saumaise was called to the scene. "Child, are you really as frightened as that? We don't want you to be hurt. Please come down and we'll talk it over."

"You'll only trick me again! I'm going to jump; and I don't care if I *am* hurt. You'll *all* be sorry."

Anne-Alexis took the rope in one slim hand and gripped a branch with the other. But she was no expert in the tying of knots. The rope slipped and she had a struggle to avoid falling. To save herself, she clutched a smaller branch which bent low under her weight. Frightened, the girl clung with both hands while the branch swayed down low under her weight, bringing her soon within reach of Mother Saumaise and some of the other sisters. By now, the child was ill with the effects of the effort and the fright. She was tucked into bed in the infirmary where Sister Margaret Mary dosed her with catnip herb tea to settle her stomach and help her to sleep.

Father Claude visited her the next day. "Well, Mademoiselle! Where did you learn to climb trees so well?"

Surprisingly, the girl had been impressed by the kind treatment she had been given. She blushed and smiled shyly at Claude, no longer the fighting young Amazon.

"Father, I had a lovely dream last night. I can't forget it. I saw myself in the most beautiful bridal garments, walking around that very tree, admiring the fruit on it. I don't know what it was supposed to show me, but I no longer feel angry or afraid."

Months later, Claude had a letter from Mother Saumaise telling that this child had received her First Holy Communion. In later years she entered the Visitation Order. She wrote that she had "never hoped nor expected to be so happy."

Another example of Claude's unusual ability to help people to understand themselves can be seen in one of the finest examples of his perception of inner qualities hidden from others. His talent was all the more notable when it is remembered that there are never two people who understand or feel alike about their religion. Marie Marguerite Rosalie de Lyonne was a very confused young woman, a native of Paray. Marie Rosalie had great natural beauty and grace. Because she had relatives in official positions throughout France, she had many opportunities for keeping up a lively social life. She frequently traveled. Her wardrobe was legendary, ranging from smart riding habits to delicate ball gowns.

She had great conceit, and thought she would never marry "any but a prince." She delighted in talking with priests, only to mildly deride their words before the conversation ended.

On one of these occasions, before Claude had arrived in Paray, a priest had remarked that the great Jesuit preacher, Father de la Colombiere, would come to Paray "to help a chosen soul." Marie preened herself in vanity, certain that hers was the chosen soul.

So, in time, Father de la Colombiere found himself a guest at a party given by Marie. He refused a cup of chocolate, which surprised his hostess, who had intended the chocolate as a compliment to his awareness of fashionable refreshment. He explained coolly that, "there is now a Jesuit ban on chocolate."

He heard much of the gossip of the guests. Helpless to put an end to it, but not wanting to seem to approve it, he walked over to a window overlooking the Bourbince River. Marie-Rosalie soon joined him there.

"Do you not approve of my party, Father?"

He looked coldly at her extravagant silk dress.

"Oh! It is I you disapprove of!" the girl cried.

"You make me think of a corpse your mother is keeping in her house."

She was horrified. "Father! How can you say such a thing?"

He looked at the young men standing about the room, all quite obviously waiting for a chance to talk with her.

"If you would spend a little of the time in prayer that you spend in trying to distract these poor youths, I could admire you. The day will come when all this will change. What will be your diversion then?"

"Father, I do not see any harm in anything I am doing. *I do not intend to be a nun.*"

"Don't be too sure of that!"

He left the party soon after this exchange.

Marie recalled, during the next few days, some of the incidents which had happened to her in the past.

There was the time she had awakened from a deep sleep. She had seen through the draperies of her bed curtains the ghost of one of her admirers who had been killed in a duel. She had heard him say, "How great God is, how just!"

Terrified at this sight, she had asked him, "How did you merit God's mercy?"

Before he had disappeared, he had said, "By my charity to the poor."

That night the color had left her face, and for the rest of her life, she was as pale as death.

She also remembered the day she had left church after Benediction of the Blessed Sacrament dressed in magnificent clothes and accompanied by the usual crowd of laughing young people. A herd of pigs came trotting down the middle of the street. Her friends stepped back to let them pass. But Marie laughed, "Let them go around me!"

The pigs did not recognize her superiority, however, and one very large animal ran straight toward her. She found herself suddenly astride the beast facing backward and unable to get off. Her friends stood on the lawn and laughed at the spectacle.

It was not so much the incident which had infuriated her; it was the letters and the bits of satiric verse which had been sent to her long afterward.

The stern words of Father de la Colombiere had their effect on the girl. His sermons seemed to be intended to challenge her way of life. It soon became her habit to lead her party guests to any church or chapel where she knew he was preaching.

Soon also, she found herself bargaining with Claude. She would not give up all for God, but she *would* give up some special dish she particularly liked. She would not go into a convent but she *would* spend certain hours in prayer.

Claude was able, in time, to say of her that "the admiration she had formerly given to her beauty she now gave to her virtue."

But her habit of selfishness was hard to change. Marie Marguerite Rosalie de Lyonne continued to try to draw Claude into her merrymaking. He didn't object to the dancing and fun, but when Marie appeared to be taunting God and when she remarked one day, "You only want me to become a Visitation nun," he replied seriously, "I wouldn't think of bringing such a disaster upon the Order or upon the Church!" This kind of challenge intrigued her.

Marie's was not the only soul to whom Claude showed a stern attitude.

When penitents complained of their trials, he often told them, "Thank God that he thinks you worthy to share his cross. Bear it with him. Do not refuse it."

It was said that Father Claude de la Colombiere's special talent was to lead souls to God.

10.

Mission to England

"WHY are the windows boarded over? And out in this room, the mice make nests in the straw of the beds. We should be able to do better than *this*, at least!"

Claude was talking to Monsieur Bouillet, a lawyer of Paray. They were exploring an old building which certainly was not at the time serving a good purpose, not even providing proper shelter for wandering gypsies. Claude thought it might be made into a hospital.

Paray-le-Monial had been a center for convents, monasteries and colleges for several hundred years. But the population at the time of Margaret Mary and Claude was largely Calvinist and Huguenot. Money for charitable works was hard to obtain from the small Catholic population. Calvinism had no confidence in public service. It was considered "money down the well."

Monsieur Bouillet explained, "Several years ago the Ladies of Charity set up a primitive hospital here with simple straw bunks. It was served by volunteer workers. Lately we have had no money, and a scarcity of volunteer helpers — a combination we have found discouraging."

Claude remarked thoughtfully, "My superiors have seen a need for a suitable hospital. We'll assume the task of finding the money."

While it was true that a hospital was greatly needed, the spiritual activities of the community had to take first place. To promote confraternity in Paray, sodalities of Mary, composed of farmers, business men and professionals, were organized by Claude. Inspired by his ideas, they gave their devoted support to working for the neglected poor. These men were convinced within a few months that a hospital could be founded to shelter the sick. The site and the means of creating a fund were then worked out. Monsieur Bouillet had in his care a small amount in alms money which would form the basis of the fund.

This work, the reorganization of the Jesuit College, as well as interest in and direction of individuals, kept Claude busy. What excitement, indeed, had he found in Paray! He felt that he could spend the rest of his life here and remain busy and interested.

One afternoon before the school vacation of 1676, Claude strolled through the country pathways from Paray to the village of Charolles, along one of the routes which had become familiar and pleasing to him. The lacy white wild carrot and the delicate pink clover sent their perfume through the June air and the scent of the tantalizing wild strawberry brought a smile to his face. Not far away, hopping about gleefully and filling their wicker baskets with colorful flowers, he could see a party of children. When he returned he found a letter on his desk from his superior. It told him, "We are thinking of opening a much greater field for your zeal and exceptional talents." The field would likely be in another part of France, he told himself. How glad he felt to know that Sister Margaret Mary found herself in a much more secure situation.

But when the assignment became definite he discovered that he was to proceed to London to be chaplain to the Duchess of York, the future Queen of England. He would have from August till October to put his affairs in order in Paray and to receive his instructions in Paris. This, then, was the special mission. Claude had been chosen by King Louis XIV himself. Pere Papon had told him that Jesuit life could be unpredictable. It was indeed!

A beautiful, bright, blazing season of the year it was to travel down to Paris! The copper and gold beeches, the silver birches, the sapphire of the Loire and the Seine delighted him. And as he rode in the coach he wondered if it could have been his father's old friend, the Duc de Villeroi, or his former employer, Colbert, who had mentioned him to the King?

A thorough briefing was given to Claude when he reached Paris. It was necessary that he should know about the secret negotiations for the friendship and possible conversion of the English King, who was secretly interested in Catholicism but was very weak. He must be told of many other matters.

King Louis' secretary spoke, "Politics in England is fraught with superstition and suspicion. When the plague struck London about ten years ago it was decided that the Catholics had brought it. The Great Fire a year later was also laid at their doorstep. Common trust and personal security are at an appallingly low level.

"Orphanages and hospitals have been closed because they were often conducted by religious groups which have been banned. No one will supply money for the helpless and the poor now. Even ordinary schooling is practically nonexistent."

"Never forget that your religion can be practiced only in private, and even then at your own risk. Your position is an official one. Any good that you can do is acceptable. But use the utmost care."

This, in brief, was the warning Claude carried with him. He had been reminded, further, that the Test Act had decimated the more able groups in England. In order to hold any position of worth in this government, one was required to swear disbelief in transubstantiation and receive communion in the Anglican church. Those who would not do so were punished by imprisonment, death, or exile. Ireland, France, and Belgium gained many of these sturdy souls as did the American colonies, some of which allowed religious freedom.

One murky, chilly morning in the middle of October, Claude was accompanied to the docks in Calais by a brother priest. He walked up the plank and introduced himself to the captain, who said he had been notified by the King's secretary of his coming.

"It needs a staunch sailor to travel the Channel passage,

Father," exclaimed the French captain of the merchantman. He looked keenly at the slim priest with the frail air and wondered how he would make out. A merchantman had no cabin boys. But there was that young apprentice, the Des Rosier boy, a neighbor of his own family. He would have had fine training at home and would watch the Father carefully.

The captain was startled to see Claude laugh and give a playful little kick to one of several wooden chests waiting to be carried below where it would be dry. "You carry silk to England, sir?"

"Yes, Father, how do you know?"

"These chests are labeled *Andre LaBelle, Silk Merchant, Lyons, France!* He is a friend of mine."

"Oh," smiling now, "yes, I take silks and wine, sometimes barrels of grain, fine dishes and glassware. Then on our return we bring iron and steel goods, cutlery, cheap print cottons, woolens, and tobacco goods which the English produce and package from their colonial trade. Yes, we're always busy."

"Where do I stay during the passage, Captain?"

"I have a small place down this way." And he led Claude between rows of chests in the hold just below deck. A sliding door opened to a cupboard-like cubicle. It had one porthole, a narrow berth and a chest.

"Here is the secret of the cabin, Father. Open the lowest compartment of the chest. Reach in and pull the leather loop behind the drawer. The covered box that comes out will hold your clerical clothes and any thing else you want returned to France. Leave a note addressing them."

"Is it necessary to be so secret?"

"Not usually; but the search for priests has come right onto our ships at times. Then, occasionally, some particular priest is being hunted down. At these times we have visitors to look over our ship. If this happens, we'll warn you and see that some of the chests hide your doorway."

Claude was already involved in intrigue! He found the idea

slightly stirring and felt the loneliness giving way to anticipation of what was to come.

Left alone, he became conscious of the rocking and swaying of the boat. He was accustomed to some travel on the French canals and on the Rhone River and he knew that this surging of the water against the hull and the squealing and creaking of the timbers and pulleys advertised a tremendous force of water and wind.

For some minutes he stared out of the porthole at the grey fog and the beating spray. Then as he looked down at the knee breeches and hose which had been laid out for him, he was appalled. A black wool surcoat and a plain waistcoat showed the unruffled stock and his linen shirt. A small, conservative hat without buckle or plume lay on the chest. "Pretty fancy clothes," he thought, "for a Jesuit."

He was to look as much like a country squire or a teacher as possible. There was a rumor of one Jesuit in England who held a job as a handyman on a farm near London. From this menial base, dressed in rustic clothing, he wandered near and far, apparently as an errand boy but secretly an apostle.

Claude, whose correspondence had been voluminous, must now remember that the smallest letter on a religious or a political theme might cause untold damage.

Thirteen hours had passed since anchor had been weighed in Calais. The captain and the young Des Rosier boy had looked in on him, bringing bread and broth and some fruit. It was now past sunset. He picked up his hat and his long, warm cloak and left the cabin for the upper deck.

A gust of wind tore at his cloak as he emerged from the hatchway. He jammed his hat down tightly and walked thoughtfully toward the starboard rail.

Claude must face the truth about his position.

In a sense, he would be unique in this poor country. It would be no secret that he was a Jesuit priest — no secret, that is, to a certain small circle of people. The King, Charles II, and his court would know, and the King's brother, James, Duke of York, as well as Mary

Beatrice, the Duchess of York, that same Mary Beatrice D'Este he had met in Lyons. He must act prudently not to violate this diplomatic appointment. He must not bring disgrace on France or on his Order.

He would say Mass in the chapel of the Duchess of York, a courtesy granted her because of her noble Italian family and her protection by France. She would be allowed to have her family in the chapel as well as non-English Catholic guests. Claude could not preach or teach in any other place except the chapel of the Duchess. He was allowed, however, to say Mass in his own quarters, alone.

He might never know why he had been chosen for this mission. But he had long ago offered his whole self to God, even if, as he had written at that time, he were to suffer "death by the executioner, prison, slander, blame, contempt, illness." And in this land of confusion where so many people were being hunted down and dealt just such blows, he knew it was quite possible for him, also, to be one of the hunted ones. Often in these days he thought of the Jesuit martyrs: Isaac Jogues, Jean de Brebeuf, Pierre Lallemont! There were heroes of this stamp in England too!

Deep in his meditation, Claude had not noticed the sailors busying themselves with ropes and anchor chains now that land had appeared on the port bow. It was time he finished his packing and placed the letters he had written today in the "secret box."

He spent that night in Dover and then progressed to a cold, wet London. Fog hung across the rooftops and over the Thames. Important drivers and rivermen shouted, "Look out! Look where you're going!" at each other. He stepped warily out of the coach and surveyed the scene.

Horses strained as they pulled heavy loads out of deep puddles of mud. He stared at the water and deep ruts in the street. How did one travel over these streets? In a few places cobblestones emerged from the general mire. He shivered and pulled his cloak tighter.

"Are you Monsieur de la Colombiere?" Claude suppressed a

grin of surprise and nodded solemnly. No priestly title would be heard here, he remembered.

"The Duchess sends you her greetings and says we are to take you to your quarters." He stepped into the sedan chair they carried on their sturdy shoulders and let down the sheltering curtain. How well these men dressed for the weather! High leather boots, long leather capes! They seemed comfortable. They took him to a building attached to St. James Palace, where he would have a small apartment.

Claude admitted to himself that life had been so eventful since he had left Lyons that he hadn't often recalled the young Duchess, Mary Beatrice. He sat down to eat the warm collation brought to him. It was while he ate that something came to mind which hadn't meant much at the time it had happened. Marie Rosalie de Lyonne had once remarked, "Mary Beatrice was always writing to her friends, the Visitation nuns, and giving them a 'rendezvous' in the sacred Side of Christ," an idea borrowed from St. Francis de Sales. He had been startled to hear this because of the analogy to Sister Margaret Mary's work. It now provided him with a valuable key to the thinking of the Duchess.

In the interval before he saw the Duchess, he resolved upon the austerities he would observe during his entire stay in London; he would sleep on a mattress on the bare floor; he would dispense with a fire in his room; he would not take advantage of permission to eat French food, but would eat the English food even if he found it heavy and unpalatable. Of these sacrifices the food was the most difficult. One restraint Claude took upon himself is quite revealing. In one of his rooms were wide windows which looked out upon the pleasant park set out between Whitehall and St. James Palace. Never, at any time while Claude inhabited that room, did he permit himself to enjoy the scene or to observe who might be walking there. He had promised himself that he would forego the use of any transportation whenever it was possible to walk. His whole being was given at all times to his mission.

Claude was able to find Father Whitbread whom he had been advised to consult, living in quiet seclusion. He had been on a mission in England on behalf of the Jesuit Order for thirty years, having been the Jesuit Provincial until the Society's expulsion from the country. He assured Claude, "There will be no success for your mission. The King is interested in the old Catholic religion of his parents, but he is weak, too easily led by politicians, and is much under their influence." Again, Claude was advised to be prudent.

The Duchess, Mary Beatrice, was a model of serenity and dignity. Her beauty was admired by even the enemies of the royal family. Many other beauties of the court scoffed at her modesty, her courtesy, and her lack of interest in the flirtations so fashionable at the time. She was deeply devoted to her husband and her sorrow in the loss of her first baby, a girl, was real and moving. James, the Duke of York, hoped for a son, but when the second child was also a girl, he showed no disappointment, for the poor little Duchess had enough trials in her life. The Duke was a noble soul. His greatest fault was that he believed all others to be as well-intentioned as he was.

Mary Beatrice had sympathy for the message of the Sacred Heart of Jesus. It was this interest which encouraged Claude to speak often of the Sacred Heart in his sermons. It was, in fact, during this period that Claude composed his "Offering to the Sacred Heart of Jesus" which he shared with his friends and the Jesuit and Visitation Orders, and which was eventually to form the basis for both the Morning Offering and the Consecration to the Sacred Heart. A few years after Claude's death, as Queen and exiled to France, the Duchess' blossoming love for the Sacred Heart prompted her to send the first royal petition to Rome begging for authorization for the establishment of the feast of the Sacred Heart.

Claude had many pleasant and interesting conversations with King Charles. There were times when the King half-promised his return to Catholicism. But it was safer for him to observe the government-approved forms and postponement followed upon delay.

Though Charles admitted to Courtin, the French ambassador, that there were still about twelve thousand Catholics in London, he still feared to show his true feelings. Claude could sympathize with this King. He could not, however, condone the extremes of joviality and excitement with which the monarch seemed to make up for this loss of freedom of conscience.

Claude had been accustomed to the sound of bells and chimes to herald the offering of Mass. In Avignon and Lyons the chimes were notable. In Paris they were expected. But here in the chapels where he might say Mass there was no such glad announcement. He prepared for each Mass in a silence broken only by the whispering and chattering of his assembling congregation.

His sermons were not long, because many who attended had other appointments to meet; he made up for this in vigorous speech and delivery.

Toward the court society's frivolous behavior Claude had a cold opinion. It was revealed in such sermons as this:

"Without those dedicated souls who pray constantly to make reparation for the pains of our Lord in the Garden of Olives, and at the pillar, and on the cross, what would we do? Is life a trinket which we will snatch without a 'thank you' to the Giver of life?"

"Your fair island of England was once inhabited by people who were inspired to love of their neighbors by perfect charity. Wandering minstrels sang of our Lord and our Lady. Prisons were almost unknown. Orphans and widows were taken in and comforted. What has become of this way of living?"

"We sometimes develop the most careless attitude toward slander. Rather than take a firm stand, we choose to condone it. Have you become accustomed to dropping remarks about this one and that one?"

"You may tell me that you spoke only to a man of prudence and discretion. Is that supposed to be comforting? I would prefer that a man of no character thought ill of me rather than a man of good standing. You might only have said that I was a priest, without further identifying me, or that I was a lawyer. Your hearers will then think less of all priests or lawyers. Words you broadcast or whisper can never be recalled. Have a care about what you say!"

"We can see how we love ourselves when we watch a fashionable lady preparing for a ball. What will she not do to be attractive! For four or five hours she will endure agony and torture. She is singed, plucked and then laced to the point of choking, then painted and powdered. After all of this, is it any wonder she is in despair if she does not gain the attention of those she sets out to attract?"

"Such extravagant dress as some people wear is unsuitable in church. What need do we have to dazzle anyone in church? It is as though Magdalene had put on her best jewels to be present at the crucifixion."

Claude saw evidence of dozing among his congregation. He remembered something from long ago, when Pere Papon, that master preacher, had dealt with this problem. He took a long breath, smiled, spread out his arms in a wide gesture, and said, "How much more she would gain if she put all this care and work into charitable undertakings!"

The smile came through his voice and he saw several people recollect themselves, blinking their eyes. He went on, "There is a little nun in a convent not too many miles away who has seen the Sacred Heart of our Lord. He has told her that he wants us to love God and our neighbor. He wants us to receive the Blessed Sacrament often. He will reward those who love him with peace of soul."

Claude was pleased when he found that these sermons were bringing sincere penitents to him. Souls which he could present to the Sacred Heart were pleasing to him. He was happy indeed.

He had noticed that there were those among his hearers who bridled at the criticism of their beauty routines or of their dress. The clutching or patting of jewels or of luxurious furs told a story to Claude's trained observation. In time, however, though some dropped away, the congregation grew and showed signs of heeding his words.

Now Claude saw two dangers. One was the danger to himself in allowing himself the happiness of success. When he had made that heroic vow before his ordination he had determined that he would remain detached from all such feelings of pride.

The second danger was one he could see for the Jesuit Order if it became noticeable that his work made converts to an outlawed religion.

Many conditions in England caused Claude great discomfort and mortification. The heavy English food was distressing to him who had been accustomed to fruits and light foods. The cold, the fog and dampness, the absence of a warming sun made him conscious of his sojourn in this cold land. Most of all, the fumes from the soft, gassy coal burning in the fireplace caused him to cough painfully.

One day on his return to his rooms, he found this note waiting for him:

Dear Father de la Colombiere,

"Can you find it possible to come to my study soon?

"I fear that my husband is in danger. In your dealings and among your acquaintances, have you met a man called Titus Oates?"

Mary Beatrice d'Este
Duchess of York"

11.

Danger

THE Duchess greeted Claude in a state of apprehension.

"I came as soon as I read your note. What is the trouble, Mary? As for Titus Oates, yes, I know he has been very active and has caused the arrest of many priests." The Duchess was alarmed. "Father! You aren't well! Let me have the Duke send his doctor to you to help that cough."

"It won't do much good, I am afraid. It is really the fault of the coal in the fireplaces. The fumes irritate my throat. I'll be all right."

Mary had been busy with a jar and a kettle of hot water. Now she handed Claude a cup of steaming, fragrant liquid, saying, "Here is a cup of tea, a brew from China. Drink it and it will refresh you and soothe your throat."

He sipped the pleasant hot drink.

"Delicious! I think I feel better already. Now what is the trouble and what does Titus Oates have to do with James?"

"Father, could Titus Oates be a madman? He is making accusations against everyone. Even Queen Catherine, who is not even a Catholic, has been accused of treason."

"This man Oates is bold, I know. He has become a coarse, crude hero in the Parliament. The accusations he makes are fit for no sensible person. He wouldn't hesitate to accuse the King. I still don't see why James of York is touched."

- 103 -

"You know that James commands the English Navy and that he has been on duty off the shores of the Low Countries; and so much of our army is in Holland fighting! Oates has accused James of keeping our fighting forces in the Low Countries so that the Jesuits can easily move, here in London, to seize the Parliament and the throne." Mary Beatrice began to weep.

Claude was really startled.

"Mary, you don't think that I propose to be King!" he teased. Even as concerned as she was, Mary Beatrice had to giggle at this.

"Come, now, what do you expect I can do about this?"

"I have written a note which will pass you into the meeting of the King's Council this afternoon. I don't know what it will accomplish, but Titus Oates has been ordered to explain his activities before Charles and the Council. If we had first-hand knowledge of this man we might obtain help from our own friends."

"I will go. But I have no hope it will come to anything except to let us see what he is really like. Yes, Mary, I will go. You pray and rest yourself. I'll let you know what happens."

There were many reasons, as Claude could see, for even decent men of England to fear these "sham" plots which a man like Titus Oates, half-educated, ignorant, and superstitious, could spread through the population. It was true that a man who owned a fine estate inherited from his father or grandfather as a bounty for services to Cromwell or an earlier leader, would listen with more attention than such talk deserved. These estates had often been convents or abbeys confiscated from the Church by Henry, Elizabeth or Cromwell. The present owner would not want to risk a return of his lands to the Church. He kept on the right side of popular opinion, which in these days was quite decidedly pro-Titus Oates!

Claude entered the chambers at Whitehall. Distinguished members of the government sat on the benches around the room. When the hearing started, Claude saw Oates for the first time. Titus Oates was a strange looking man. His neck was so short one could scarcely determine whether he had one. His forehead was ignobly tiny. His face had a flat appearance.

At one time in the hearing he exclaimed in a threatening manner to King Charles, "Your Majesty, I talked to Don Juan, Prince of Spain. He told me he has promised to help the Jesuits to overthrow you. I guess everybody will listen to me when that happens!" he roared. A stir of shocked surprise could be heard throughout the chamber.

King Charles recognized the falsehood here and asked, "What does Don Juan look like?"

Titus Oates thought quickly. Don Juan was Spanish, so he improvised, "He is a tall man, very thin and dark."

Charles sprang to his feet in anger and slammed the table with his hands, shouting, "Don Juan is short and stout and is very blonde! You are not telling the truth!"

Claude was not the only one in the chamber who expressed amazement that a man would so boldly lie to promote his own schemes. After the hearing ended, Oates left, still scowling and muttering to himself, discredited for the present time.

Claude departed quietly, knowing that this crisis was far from over. This man would never cease to work his evil deeds. He lived to see lives ruined and to cause blood to flow. He had just the right talent for sly whispering, and his threats trapped the insecure into compliance.

Claude felt an admiration for Charles he had never expected to give this weak man. At least, Charles had shown a contempt for falsehood and he could mock Oates for this false plot. To find these marks of character in Charles lifted his heart somewhat.

Discouragement had often overtaken Claude during his years in England. He had felt physical and mental discomforts which had pressed sternly upon him.

Criticism he had suffered from another priest had been particularly oppressive, almost causing him to resign and return to France. It had come from a priest who didn't agree with Claude's teaching about the Sacred Heart. The man's inclination to a cold attitude towards the Blessed Sacrament was offended by the request of Jesus for frequent communion. Sister Margaret Mary wrote to Claude and told him that God had revealed to her that Claude was troubled. He was not to resign. He was to ignore the criticism. "You traveled to England knowing you would meet danger, did you not?" she reminded him.

Claude's teaching about the divine Heart made it clear that the Heart of Christ was not only a fleshly one, but also spiritual, that this Heart was the origin of all love and the refuge to which all the world might fly.

Political strife often touched closely upon Claude's existence here in England, as it had sometimes seemed to do in France, but physical danger really meant little to him. His interior pains gave him more trouble, from which he knew no rest.

Doubts of his own worthiness assailed him perpetually. A spiritual retreat at this time was to help him give consideration to the state of his soul. He wrote that he was less inclined to vainglory over his accomplishments: "This knowledge of myself is a miracle which God alone could work in me."

But he revealed that Margaret Mary had sent him a memorandum of helpful advice when he had departed for England. In this London retreat of eight day's duration, he went through the points brought out in the paper. He found he could now understand them as applied to his life, where they had formerly been quite puzzling to him. Experience with the difficulties of the English had given him a new insight into himself. And, resolving once more to leave all in the hands of God, he determined to do all in his power to establish devotion to the Sacred Heart of Jesus wherever he might be.

The chase after Jesuit missionaries had been more or less active in recent years, depending on the scares such as the Titus Oates incident. Would he become involved in this side of the English scene? That this was truly the beginning of a persecution of the Church, Claude had no doubt. He had, long ago, and even recently, offered his "all." Would he be found worthy to join that noble company of Jean de Brebeuf, Isaac Jogues, and Edmund Campion, those valiant martyrs?

One friend, in speaking of his own flight from pursuers, had said, "I spent two days and two nights in a little chimney hole where I was able to move only a few inches."

"Why did you stay there? Why didn't you leave when you found the house under surveillance?"

"The soldiers had already camped on the lawn and there were guards at the doors and on the stairway at all times. I was lucky, though. The housewife used to put some biscuits, cheese, and fruit with a jug of fresh water on a little shelf. A small beam of light came through a chink high up in the wall. I had to stand or sit in a cramped position. Some of us have not been so fortunate!"

If Claude had any doubts about the aroused feelings of the general population, he was undeceived by a frightening encounter as he returned one day from a visit to a sick man.

Walking up a narrow street he caught sight of some confusion ahead. A crowd of people surged toward him.

Jostling mobs pushed back and forth along the street. The noise of shouting and laughing was deafening. Claude found a shop entrance where he could stand and watch.

"Pretty rough, aren't they?" Claude remarked to the shopkeeper as he came to the door.

"No, it's the celebration of the Fifth of November Gunpowder Plot. It's like this every year. Here they come now — see the puppets up the street?"

High up in the air dangled life-sized figures representing a Pope and two Cardinals dressed in tawdry cambric robes and fitted with grotesque, leering masks. A mocking crowd paraded with this display.

The expression of repugnance that overcast Claude's bland face was involuntary. It was noticed by the shopkeeper.

"Where are they going?" Claude asked. He wondered if this could be a budding riot such as he had once seen in Avignon.

"They go to Smithfield Market where they'll burn the effigies."

Claude had his feelings in check by now, his face calm and his thoughts collected. Above the din there came a wild, piercing screech and wail, a snarl and a shriek. The old man chuckled. Claude turned on him with a look of anger. "What is that?"

The man took Claude's arm and pulled him into the shop. Behind the mirthless chuckle Claude now saw disgust in his eyes.

"Don't mind it, lad. 'Tis nothing you can help. Ye're French —or Flemish? Come in here."

"I'm from France." Involuntarily, Claude made the sign of the cross.

"Ah, yes! Well, let me tell you. My name is Smith. But it was not always Smith. It used to be Stuart. Back in the time of Cromwell my father could get no business with such an unpopular name so when we moved across the city we became Smith. My great-grandfather was cousin to Mary Stuart."

"Do you ever hear Mass?"

" 'Tis against the law. Those who know where to go are pretty careful. It's dangerous to expose a whole group to arrest for one stranger like me!"

Claude talked a while, and promised to see Smith again and to arrange for the sacraments for him.

"But why do they put cats in those puppets?"

"They blamed Mary for the Gunpowder Plot, you know, though we Stuarts knew differently. The mob likes to imagine the Pope and Cardinals screaming when the puppets burn."

"Poor cats! Poor mob!" exclaimed Claude. "It's easy to fool them out of their souls."

Later Claude approached the Palace drive. At the gate a small sedan chair carried by two porters had been shoved aside by the crowd. Claude heard from the chair, "Monsieur Colombiere! Monsieur! I would like to talk with you."

The gatekeeper was opening the gates and the porters carried the chair inside. They set it down and stepped back so that Claude could talk.

A young woman inside the chair began, "I am the Lady Ann, a lady-in-waiting to Queen Catherine."

"Ah, yes! I have seen you at the court. I think I have seen you at Mass."

"Yes, you have, Father. That is why I want to talk to you."

"My grandparents were exiled to Ireland because they refused to take the Oath. They would not change their religion. My parents live in Ireland now, where I was brought up. I am here because I was appointed to the court with the help of a relative with a position at court. I would have married James de Warren, also the son of an exiled family, when he returned from the wars in Holland. But James was killed a few weeks ago.

"I shall not stay now. I would like to enter the Visitation Order to which Sister Margaret Mary belongs. I am asking you and the Duchess of York to help me to arrange this."

Claude saw sincerity in the girl's manner. "Are you certain of this or is it just because of your present loneliness that you ask it?"

"I am serious, Father. This is what I want. But we must not talk longer. The porters are beginning to be curious. Will you help, Father?"

"I will, Lady Ann. I'll do all that I can do, and you will hear from the Duchess soon."

Claude walked on to the entrance. The porters picked up the chair and followed. It came to him that even in this cold country there were people who struggled against intrigue, treachery, deprivation of freedom, who had the greatness to make the ultimate oblation of their lives.

This thought brought to mind another, for as he walked through the shining halls he recalled Mary Ward, who had lived about forty years ago in a slum district of London. She had been appalled at the plight of orphans who, having no place to go, would search garbage heaps for food and would find places to sleep in horse or cow barns where the heat from the animals would keep them from freezing.

Mary Ward had gathered other widows and lonely women together. They made up a rule for their lives. They had no religious habit and usually no priest to guide them (except for an occasional fugitive who would say Mass for them).

They had rescued many a child from a life of crime. Each child was taught to keep house or tend a garden, to groom a horse, polish harnesses or perform any other suitable service that would make it possible for him to earn a living.

Though Mary Ward had died, her followers still carried on the work in the St. Martin's Lane building. Claude had often visited them and provided money for food.

Last week he had a surprise visit from Father Wall, one of the most admired fugitive priests. Father Wall had come in the disguise of an old, stooped, lame man leaning on a cane. It was only after he and Claude were certain that no one would enter Claude's apartment again that evening that he had thrown aside his disguise and told Claude who he was. They had shared Claude's supper. Father Wall had stayed for the night and had said Mass at Claude's altar.

And the news he had brought had filled Claude with joy. The old priest had been in Belgium and had heard many priests talk about the Sacred Heart and about Sister Margaret Mary Alacoque's visions.

"Keep on writing your letters whenever you can get them through, Claude. They reach far and wide!" were Father Wall's words at parting.

Claude smiled at the jubilant feeling that came when he thought of this growing devotion.

He opened the door to his rooms after Father Wall had left and sat down at his desk. Suddenly he was seized with a spasm of coughing. He felt a gush of warm blood rush to his lips. When he held his handkerchief to his mouth, it was undeniably stained. Here, in this moment, Father Claude was certain of his fate.

He wrote to Sister Margaret Mary Alacoque, "Mother Saumaise has written to me that you have had great and distressing difficulties. Your sufferings must be regarded as a share of the sufferings of our Lord. They are terribly discouraging, but there is, you must believe, a reason for it.

"As for me, have no fear that I will come to the hangman's noose as so many of my brother priests here are doing. This fate I shall cheat. Today I became certain that my ignominious end will be death by tuberculosis!"

12.

The Mysterious Rejection

FOG pressed and rolled against the windows of Claude's room where he knelt reciting the litany to our Lady for the "poor, misled people of England and for all those who suffered." It was the early morning of November 24, 1678. Outside his door stood the guards who had kept him under house arrest for a few days. He was not alarmed, but saw that a change in his life could be near.

Then the tread of heavy boots pounded on the stairway outside. Before the next "Pray for us," his door burst open and without ceremony he was told to prepare to leave for prison.

"Come with us!"

"I'll need to have my cloak," Claude protested, reaching toward his cloak hanging near the door.

"Don't you pull away from me, you Jesuit plotter! You probably want to get your sword."

Claude would have felt more like laughing at this ridiculous remark if the men hadn't been so deadly serious.

"Aw, let 'im get 'is cloak; it can't make any difference," drawled another soldier, to whom Claude felt eternally grateful.

When he reached for the cloak Claude was able to snatch his breviary from a nearby shelf and, in the gloom of early morning, tuck it into an inside pocket.

If only he could chance to meet someone of the Duchess'

household in the hallway — or one of James' staff — or, if he could get a message to Charles; but they met nobody in the hallways at that early hour; no rescue was in sight.

The street outside was deep in mud, filth, and odorous refuse; in late November after the fall rains, the streets were different from other times of the year only in being dirtier and not yet frozen. Luckily, the soldiers' cart was used to carry him to King's Bench Prison.

"Where's yur fee?" was the question posed to him at the prison gatehouse.

"Fee? You charge a fee of prisoners?" Claude asked in amazement.

"Certainly. It costs money to keep a roof over yur heads," the plump man with a large red nose whined virtuously. Claude's money pouch had been in his cloak, and he was able to pay the prison fee and a fee for food which the man also demanded.

He was hustled into a dark, dingy, damp room containing people of a vast assortment. There were no chairs, only heaps of straw were piled here and there. "This must be an outer waiting room or cell," thought Claude. "They will take me to another place later."

Long past midday a man came in carrying a basket of bread chunks and a pail of water having a single dipper. He tossed a chunk of bread to each inmate, banged the pail down on a shelf and took the empty one away.

This, Claude thought, would be their meal for today. It was. But in thinking that he would be removed to a better cell, he was disappointed. At night he had only to wrap his cloak around himself and lie on one of the dirty piles of straw. This was his simple pallet as long as he was in prison.

He, who had slept on hand-loomed linen in his mother's house; on coarse, clean brown linen in the seminary; and on soft china silk in Colbert's home, now slept on straw. Straw makes a sweet bed, a bed, he thought, fit for the Infant Savior. But this filth! How could he endure this hardship? Clearly, there was some need in this pitiable land for such immolation, for his living prayer. As Catherine of Siena had been told that the future of the entire Church depended upon her prayers and sacrifices, now he would offer this condition for whatever need there was. The Sacred Heart knew what he wanted from Claude's suffering. Let that knowledge suffice.

And so he offered the darkness, the dampness and the cold of this unsanitary place daily to the Sacred Heart. He offered his pain at hearing the grumbling and impolite speech on all sides. Most of all he grieved to be deprived of the Mass.

Many hours were passed in reviewing the thoughts he had had during his retreat in January of 1677. He remembered, "He never fails us within the limits of our needs. I am determined to place no limits to my confidence and to extend it to everything. God is a shield which covers me on all sides. You must be my strength under all crosses." During these days of ignominious imprisonment, mental prayer and meditation were his one consolation.

He had given up hope of being remembered when one day a messenger from the Duchess was able to bribe his way in to see Claude for a few minutes.

"There is nothing the Duchess can do just now. The Duke and the King are both under pressure from the Cromwellian clique and are being checked in every move."

"Alfred, do you know who had me arrested?"

"It was Oliver Fiquet. Do you know him? He was paid a reward. He has quite a lot of money to spend these days."

"The thirty pieces are symbolic, Alfred!" Claude mused.

"Thirty pieces, Father?" puzzled the man.

"I had obtained work for him because he didn't have food, Alfred. In France, his father was a herdsman on one of my mother's farms, years ago."

"And this is how he repays you, Father! But I must go now. I'll try to come in again in two days. If you can write any letters I'll take them to the Duchess to have them sent through."

But little could be done yet to help Claude. He was ill, fevered, cold, hungry, and tortured by his surroundings. He knew that his teachings on the Sacred Heart were responsible for this perilous position. Perhaps the coveted crown of martyrdom was, after all, within his grasp. Several priests he had known had been executed. Surely it would come now to him!

Christmas came and went. Claude had only his memories and his inner thoughts to help him observe the day of the Holy Nativity.

One day soon after Christmas there came an unusually cold day. Claude huddled, shivering, in a corner.

"Oh! Oh-h-h-h!" A low moan sounded near him in a very dark corner. Claude wondered what ailed the man. He moved closer to try to talk. Just then an ugly, beady-eyed rat hurtled out of a dismal corner and ran across the man's feet.

A whisper came to Claude's ears, "Mary, Mother of God, help!"

"Is there anything I can do for you?" asked Claude, and he frowned, thinking how little he could do for anyone.

The man looked at him for the first time. It was not wise to talk. There could be an informer even in prison.

Claude reassured him, "I heard your prayer. I am a Catholic priest. Perhaps I could give you some help."

The man studied Claude's face long and steadily, wanting to believe him, but afraid to trust him.

Claude spoke again, "This pain that we suffer is only for a little while. Do not be afraid. If you are brought to trial and condemned, they can do no more to you. And, after all, isn't that what they did to our Lord?"

After a while he went on, "Let me tell you something. Over in France, at Paray-le-Monial, a young nun has talked with the Sacred Heart of Jesus. She has seen him. He has promised untold rewards to us. All we need to do is offer all our works and pains to his Sacred Heart. We shall not be helpless if he is with us."

The man listened with a new peace, and joy showed on his face. He told Claude, "Father, my son is in Belgium, studying. He will be ordained next year. Perhaps my trials will be a help to him and give him courage to do his work."

"If you ever find yourself free again," said Claude, "I would like you to do me a favor. Near St. Paul's Cathedral in St. Martin's Lane you will be able to find an old building where a woman named Mary Ward started a community to help people. Do what you can for them. They need us desperately."

"Father, I don't expect to leave here, but I shall help if I can, or pass the word along to one who can."

Next day Claude was called to court to be sentenced. Diplomatic letters had arrived from France concerning his case. He was taken, in his abject state, before the court. Banishment was pronounced upon him. He must *never* return to England.

Sent back to prison, he endured several more days of filth and cold. Then ten days were allowed him to rest and regain enough strength to travel. Scant mercy, but it *was* mercy!

King Charles was grieved not to have been able to assist him, for he had admired this young Jesuit.

The Duke and Duchess of York suffered also. They were exiled to Belgium.

Father Claude made his way in the bitter winter weather to Dover. A galleon from France lay in the harbor and the captain agreed to take him to Calais. He left England, "a land of crosses."

A young French sailor on the deck of the boat gave Claude an inquisitive look. Claude knew of the pale, drawn visage seen by the youth, but he couldn't know that regret and grief showed there, also.

"Somebody lives there you don't want to leave, Monsieur?"

"Many somebodies, my son, many!"

"That country is not for me. Each time I make this trip I am glad I don't have to live there.

"You should be thankful you can go back home, Monsieur, and that you are not a Jesuit priest. It has been very bad for them. Many have been tortured by the most terrible means. And to those, add at least one hundred forty-six who have died in prison."

Claude was astounded.

So many of his brothers in the Order had paid such a high price! Why should he, Father de la Colombiere, be here now? The sickness he suffered and the position he had held should have made him an easy target — either one should have prevented his release.

How often he had offered himself as a sacrifice, only now to be rejected!

Sighing deeply, he turned away and remarked, "Some of us must have special friends!"

Then the boy knew the answer to the question he had asked of the Monsieur, this priest, this rejected sacrifice!

Claude told himself he must be resigned. Perhaps "exile" from that land which needed workers, the disgrace of dismissal, the interruption of the mission, were his own special martyrdom — secret, between him and God, known to no other. Isn't that what he had asked for?

13.

To Paray and Home

THE chamber where Claude rested in Calais was far different from the resting place he had used in the past many weeks. Clean, curtained, and pleasant, it was heated by a cheering wood fire burning in the small fireplace. The housewife brought him broth and custard and tempting meals as if she were determined to make him well in the few days he could delay here.

The cold January wind from the Channel whined around the corners of the house while Claude rested. He could image the efforts of the elderly priest who had been sent to accompany him to Dijon. He was out there, plodding against this bitter wind, searching for a carriage which could carry Claude comfortably in his present weakened state.

It was useless to think of traveling on the canals, frozen in this unusual winter.

Frozen, rutted, rough roads would take a terrible toll on his strength, so the carriage must be well-sprung, large and cushioned. There would have to be curtains to shut out the bitter air. Not many families could afford to own such a vehicle.

At last one was found and equipped with cushions, blankets, hot bricks for his feet and hands and a careful driver. Claude was carried on his route by way of Paris and Lyons to Dijon. He was forced to stay over for a rest frequently, and it seemed that the story of his experiences had gone before him, for the welcomes were hearty and the questions many — more than he had the strength to answer.

There was time for endless thought and meditation at the Jesuit College des Godrans in Dijon. Not far away was the Visitation convent where Mother Saumaise was now mistress of novices. Groups of priests and brothers sought inspiration from him. Mother Saumaise brought classes of novices with whom he shared his experiences. In years to come these young nuns would have serious responsibilities. Knowing this holy priest, so full of wisdom, would give them greater insight.

Soon the journey to Paray-le-Monial had to be faced, and it taxed the last ounce of his energy. Even the scenery proved bleak, since the road meandered through the sleeping vineyards of the Cote d'Or. The black and red soil supported leafless grapevines. Only a few people moved about in the cold which was pointed out by the snow-topped mountains glistening in the distance.

After Claude had arrived in Paray and had rested for a few weeks, a piece of unfinished business — the foundation of the hospital — needed to be revived. Claude's extreme illness was the spur which aided in collecting more generous funds for this work.

Margaret Mary welcomed renewed conversations with Claude. The new superior, Mother Greyfie, had a strong aversion to new devotions and to "visions." She had forbidden the Holy Hour and had kept Margaret Mary under constant obedience. Mother Greyfie was diligently supplying the mortification which, along with constant union with God's will, ardent love and perfect humility were molding this young woman into a saint. Mother Greyfie's greatest cruelty was that she humiliated Margaret Mary publicly and involved Claude in her detractions.

Claude cared nothing for himself, but he could not let Margaret Mary's work for the Sacred Heart, so immeasurably great, undergo this harm, so he decided to speak. He convinced the superior that she was really sinning against the light of the Holy Spirit in suppressing this work. This was to be the last effort Claude would exert in

Margaret Mary's behalf. From now on, Margaret Mary would find the strength to guide her own work.

This continuing activity which gathered about Claude was tiring to him. The environment was at fault, since it contained the people, whom he could not refuse, and the work which had occupied him so fully a few years ago and still held his interested concern. The solution was sought by sending him from Paray to his native village of St. Symphorien d'Ozon. It had been thirty years since he had left this pleasant, happy home — when his family had moved down to Vienne on the Rhone River.

The house at St. Symphorien was now kept by Humbert, whose children ran about and laughed and played as merrily as he and his brothers had. Humbert often went down to Vienne on business. He would take the boys with him, for Uncle Archdeacon Floris lived in Vienne. After their return from such an excursion, Claude and Humbert always relived old memories when they heard the children bragging of their exploits in hiking up Mount Salamont. Strange as it was to Claude to be once more part of a lively family, he found himself more relaxed than he had been in years. He even coughed less on many days. They were good days for Claude except for his feeling of uselessness.

Claude's sister wrote frequently from her convent, receiving brotherly sermons in return. In these early years of the devotion to the Sacred Heart, she had some of the first precious knowledge from her brother. Young Joseph still studied diligently in Paris. In a few years he would be sent to Canada as a missionary.

Though feeling improved in strength, Claude gave the appearance of a very sick man. Resting was a severe problem to him at times. Lying down, he often had trouble with breathing. He refused to recline, so he was propped up with cushions. He demanded to sit in a chair, upright, and often spent hours struggling for breath.

These pitiful sufferings he offered to the Sacred Heart with the particular intention of union with the sufferings of Christ on the cross.

On one of these days when Claude had been in particular discomfort, he was surprised to have a visitor. Marie Marguerite Rosalie de Lyonne came into Humbert's house and seeing his suffering, threw herself at Claude's feet, overcome by his appearance, obviously feeling a great emotion. She offered to do "anything."

Claude said, "My daughter, if Christ asked for you as his bride, would you refuse?"

She would not refuse. After a year she entered the convent at Paray-le-Monial.

The disease with which Claude suffered had its phases of seeming health and collapse. It was during one of the better periods that he was recalled to Lyons. Small tasks were assigned in keeping with his strength. But the day came when he was again sent to Paray because of the winter fogs and mists in Lyons.

But in Paray his condition failed to improve. Now the perpetual inactivity began to be a burden too heavy to ignore. There was little hope of recovery and no chance of return to action soon. Being dedicated to his work, he found that idleness was the greatest suffering. It was another martyrdom.

Continually haunting him was the recollection of the disaster of his mission in England. It was a source of shame to feel that he had failed when King Louis had trusted and recommended him. He knew that his mission had been to try as unobtrusively as possible to bring about greater understanding between France and England and the Church. Charles had put him off, he reasoned, rendering his assignment ineffectual. Would unity have been served if Charles had embraced the Catholic religion? Whether this could have come about or not, Claude still felt himself at fault.

Nor, though he knew his behavior and demeanor in England had been far above reproach, had he been able to reach the masses of people who still longed for the sternly repressed Church. He wrote in agony that to have "held in his hands the fairest hopes in the world" and to have returned with his hands empty, was the greatest of humiliations. He reminded himself that he had made the heroic vow, "to accept all." Difficult as it was, he accepted the burden which seemed about to crush him.

What was it that Pere Papon had said long ago? "Who of us will run up the hill on the shores of the Mohawk River? Who of us will run the 'gauntlet' for our Lord?"

What hills had Claude run upon, he wondered; the long, tortuous trail of the conquest of self? And the gauntlet? What of criticism, of misunderstanding, calumny, chains, illness? And yet, how little this was to offer the precious Sacred Heart of Jesus!

The great Pere de la Chaise, King Louis' chaplain and advisor in matters religious, had tried to comfort Claude upon a recent visit to assure him that he had been caught up in a frenzied wave of intrigue, a condition certainly not of Claude's seeking, and one which he should not take so to heart.

The truth was that the indecision of Charles had prolonged the suffering. It would always be so, for as it was well known that Edmund Campion had suffered in England from the indecision of Elizabeth, the hunted ones of Claude's day were doomed by Charles' hidden desire for the old religion and his timidity in declaring it, either publicly or privately.

"What has my life accomplished?" Claude thought many times. He remembered the night when soldiers had stopped at their old home in Vienne. His mother and father and, in fact, the boys, had worked and given food, fuel and services to the tired, hungry and wounded men. He remembered, too, asking his mother, "Didn't they even say, 'Thank you'?"

His mother, in her sensible way, had replied that everyone says thank you in some way, and even if this is lacking, that God always does.

Claude thought that he had achieved nothing very spectacular, but he had, by his obedience to his Rule and his vow, given spiritual food, the fuel of Love, and the service of advice to many whom he had been able to reach, He had really tried. And had he not even offered his failures and disappointments?

Yes, he could still leave all in the hands of God.

And in this fear of unworthiness, his complete failure (as he thought) in all things, his inability to continue the smallest work, even to saying Mass, how very great was the virtue of trusting the rest to God!

Physical suffering was always present, as well. His family thought Vienne would give him the bracing air he needed. Floris obtained a carriage in which he would be transported. It was planned that he would leave Paray on the feast of St. Francis de Sales.

Margaret Mary sent Claude an urgent note, saying, "He told me that he wishes the sacrifice of your life in this country." Puzzled, Claude nevertheless delayed.

His family in Vienne and nearby St. Symphorien awaited his arrival so that they might tend him in his need. A few days slid by.

Then a messenger delivered a letter addressed to Humbert in St. Symphorien. It was from Claude's superior, Father Bourguignet, and Humbert read, in part, "Father de la Colombiere suffered his last attack on Sunday, February 15, in this year of our Lord, 1682. He retained his thirst for the hidden life until the very last."

In Paray, Margaret Mary had been told at five o'clock in the morning of the death of her spiritual director. She said, "Pray, and have prayers said for the repose of his soul." It had been revealed to her that Claude had needed to spend some hours in Purgatory for the fault of some hesitation in making a decision upon one occasion. Later, at ten o'clock, she told her sisters, "Don't grieve any more. Pray to him. Fear nothing; he is more powerful to help you now than ever."

If Claude had wanted to be "the man whom no one thought of any more," as he had once expressed it, he succeeded. For his superior wrote to Humbert many months later, "I have examined the statement put down by our chronicler at the time of Father Claude's death that he has nothing to report of him. Our records of events and progress in each house are sent to Rome every three years to be placed in the archives of the Society of Jesus.

"I have today, however, examined some of the manuscripts of your brother's writings on the Spiritual Retreat. He left these to us as a record of his method of teaching young seminary students. He had worked on revising and gathering these as long as he was able. We are continuing the work. We believe that they will number several volumes when counted with his reflections and his sermons. We will try to have them published by next year.

"What a help these papers will be to future priests only time can show. Upon their publication, our annals may show more than the present statement of nothing to report for the year of 1682!

"Will you and all of Claude's family join us in reading often the Offering to the Sacred Heart which Claude gave to many of us as a meditation?"

Humbert folded the letter and stood looking into the distant east where the top of Mount Salamont could be seen.

Slowly, he turned, and slowly he walked home.

Bibliography

Anderson, R. G. *Story of a Cathedral*. Longmans.

Belloc, Hillaire. *Characters of the Reformation*. Sheed and Ward.

Belloc, Hillaire. *Cromwell* Lippincott.

Belloc, Hillaire. *A History of England*. Putnam.

de la Bedoyere, Michael. *Francois de Sales*. Harper.

Farrow, John. *Pageant of the Popes*. Sheed and Ward — Catechetical Guild.

(Grenoble Ed. translation) Letters and Retreats. *Faithful Servant.* Herder.

Guitton, S.J., Georges. *Perfect Friend*. Herder.

Hughes, Phillip. *A Popular History of the Catholic Church*. MacMillan.

Talbot, S.J., Francis X. *Saint Among the Hurons*. Harper.

Talbot, S.J., Francis X. *Saint Among Savages*. Harper.

Williams, Margaret. *The Sacred Heart in the Life of the Church*. Sheed and Ward.

Yeo, Margaret. *These Three Hearts*. Bruce.